D1738690

TARPON QUEST

BOOKS BY **JOHN N. COLE**

In Maine

From the Ground Up (with Charles Wing)

Striper

Amaranth

Cityside/Countryside (with Nathan Cobb)

The Sun Book

Salmon

Breaking New Ground (with Charles Wing)

Fishing Came First

Tarpon Quest

TARPON QUEST

John N. Cole

LYONS & BURFORD, PUBLISHERS

© *1991 by John N. Cole*

ALL RIGHTS RESERVED. No part of this book may
be reproduced in any manner without the express
written consent of the publisher, except in the case
of brief excerpts in critical reviews and articles. All
inquiries should be addressed to: Lyons & Burford,
Publishers, 31 West 21 Street, New York, NY 10010

> *The decorative headpiece*
> *of a leaping tarpon*
> *used for each chapter opening*
> *was drawn especially for this book by*
> RICHARD HARRINGTON

Printed in the United States of America

10 9 8 7 6 5 4 3 2 1

Typography by Fisher Composition Inc.

Library of Congress Cataloging-in-Publication Data

Cole, John N., 1923–
    Tarpon quest/John N. Cole.
        p.   cm.
    ISBN 1-55821-097-0
    1. Tarpon fishing—Florida—Florida Keys.
    2. Saltwater fly fishing—Florida—Florida Keys.
    3. Cole, John N., 1923–
    I. Title.
    SH691.T2C65   1991
    799.1'755—dc20   90-19270
                                                CIP

FOR **JOHN GRAVES**
Who gave me the will and the way

ONE

The one place in the Florida Keys where you can count on being able to see wild tarpon swimming free is just a few steps from the Overseas Highway—that narrow ribbon of arching bridges and two-lane road that spans more than one hundred miles of islands, mangrove hammocks, and the most fascinating fishing waters in the nation. Driving "down" the Keys from Largo to Key West after you leave Islamorada and cross the Lignum Vitae Bridge, watch for the turnoff to your right at Mile Marker 77.5; it's the very first turnoff you can make in Lower Matecumbe.

There is a sign that says "Fresh Fish & Lobster" and another that says "Boats For Rent," but nothing about tarpon. The place is called "Robbie's" and, as marinas go in South

Florida and the Keys, it is a modest enterprise with a direct, no-frills approach to its daily business: buying, selling, and shipping fish and other seafoods from a small packing house; serving fish and chips, stone crabs, and lobster dinners from a decidedly informal outdoor cooking shed; renting well-seasoned Boston Whalers, Makos, and other assorted small craft to anglers, divers, and adventurers who happen by. Robbie's dock is narrow; its well-weathered wooden pilings tilt a bit and its strictly functional sun-bleached silver planking curls and splits at its edges.

But at the dock's end where a gas pump waits to fuel Robbie's rental fleet and his regular customers, the tarpon gather. At high tide, if you sit at the planking's edge, your feet will swing just a few inches above fifteen, or twenty, or perhaps as many as thirty great fish turning lazily in the clear waters of Florida Bay, gliding into the shadows beneath the dock, then reappearing, catching bits of sunlight in their iridescent scales.

They make a stunning assembly, these creatures that speak of pre-history even as they communicate elemental grace, fluid within fluid, somnolent yet charged. Some are giants, close to seven feet, awash in their own awesome girth. Others pivot more quickly, profligates spending youth's energies. Like migrant souls of the sea the tarpon appear and disappear without haste, sliding back and forth through their veil of waters in this most unlikely spot to witness a silver enchantment.

One of the giants among them has a disfigured cheek—not a

shocking scar but enough of an anomaly to draw the eye of a careful observer when the great fish rolls on its side. The several, intricate bony lines that curve to define the etched and embossed exterior anatomy of a tarpon's chitinous gill plates have been wrenched from their original symmetry. A section of the plate flares in perpetual disharmony, torn from its moorings in an earlier mishap and untended since.

It is a scar of capture. The giant took an angler's hook several years ago, was boated and then released with the wrench that tore that hook from its mouth and gills. Perhaps too traumatized to leave the waters around the dock, the ailing tarpon was tossed fish heads, guts, racks, and tails: by-products of Robbie's fish processing and marketing enterprise. As the months passed and the free food kept coming each day, the fully recovered resident fish was joined by others. What communication prompted these meetings is a mystery; the small cove at Robbie's dock is not typical of the waters tarpon seek. Nor are these sedentary creatures. They are not by nature the sheep of the seas; they are more wild bird than fish in their migratory restlessness, flowing in silver rivers through dark oceans on voyages triggered by the ancient compulsions of survival: water temperature, food, and optimum conditions for reproduction and the eternal continuation of the species.

Nevertheless, at least twenty, and perhaps more, tarpon stepped out of the ranks of their teeming wild schools and took up residence within earshot of the Overseas Highway in the small patch of Florida Bay at the end of Robbie's dock. Like the creatures themselves, first one and then more human visitors began stopping by merely to observe the awesome assembly. Then one of those observers, on the dock to watch the daily feeding, asked permission to help toss tidbits into the gleaming tarpon turmoil at their feet.

Expanding yet again on his ventures as a restaurateur, marina captain, and seafood merchant, Robbie put up a hand-lettered wooden sign at the landward end of the dock informing all comers that due to increasing demand and the rising costs of maintaining the herd, each visiting observer would be charged $1.50. The fee includes a bucket (if requested) with a few chunks of fish parts collected at the cleaning boards where yellowtail, mangrove snapper, wahoo, dolphin, kingfish, grouper, and scores of the countless other varieties of sea creatures are prepared each day for the balance of their journey to the region's dinner tables.

For anyone with the merest sliver of interest in the lives around us, that $1.50 is the investment of the century. Like a sorcerer's wand, a bit of yellowtail flesh dropped into the sea at the end of Robbie's dock transforms the assembly and galvanizes what had been a circling ballet set to slow music of the spheres. Instead of grace, there is ferocity; instead of indolence, there is quickness too fast to follow; instead of assumed domesticity, there is an unmistakeable wildness, a feral response at once so fast and so merciless that watching it seems almost an invasion of the tarpon's privacy.

4

For anglers who have tried to entice wild tarpon to take a lure, especially a fly, there is much to be learned from the vantage Robbie's dock allows. Do the fish turn on their sides to engulf their snack? Do they merely open their great maw mouths and inhale? Does their feeding become a heedless frenzy, prompting (an angler hopes) compulsive strikes: the sort of behavior that can lead to swallowing a few feathers lashed to a small hook?

Even after five or six buckets, when even the most casual observer can tell these tarpon are sated—for the moment—the questions cannot be answered. Or can be. Because, yes, some fish do roll on their sides, the sea-green of their broad backs transformed to the great sheet of gleaming silver that is their deep side, a torso so wide and so bright that turned in the clarity of shoal water it catches and holds the entire southern sky, reflecting cumulus, cerulean blue, and the essence of a midday sun, blazing more blindingly from the flashing tarpon's silver scales than from the heavens above.

There! an observer's consciousness shouts. There! That's how they take a fly. That sudden submerged sunbeam of the tarpon's reflected side—that's what the guides mean when they say, "One flashed! One flashed your fly! Did you see it?"

But then, beneath your sneakered feet swinging as you sit at the very edge of Robbie's dock, a six-foot tarpon swallows a snapper morsel with an all but invisible opening and closing of the fish's odd undershot mouth—that unmistakeable tarpon mouth with the protruding lower jaw that all but encloses its

5

upper counterpart. This tarpon never rolls, never varies its perfect vertical. No, it pushes straight ahead, the jaws open and shut all but invisibly. Did they? It happens so fast, you tell yourself, you really can't be certain. But the morsel is gone.

Is this the way tarpon take a fly? If so, then they do not roll. There are, you discover, no certainties. Because no sooner have you determined (in your neurotic quest for order, for some sort of supremacy, for some pitiful angler's advantage with these mystery creatures) that, yes, tarpon sometimes roll when they eat, and, yes, they also sometimes come straight on and gulp, but yet another alternative is demonstrated. Just when you had begun to be convinced that no matter how they take their food, all tarpon eat with the speed of light: one millisecond the food is there; the next it's gone.

But here is a tarpon toying, nudging its appropriated morsel through the water with its protruding lips shut tight, pushing first this way, then that, the way an infant in a high chair might slide a bit of buttered toast aimlessly back and forth across a shiny tray. Is this how a tarpon reacts to a lure, with this elaborate indolence, a kind of noble ennui? If so, then anglers can find no cause for hope.

Spend half an hour at the end of Robbie's dock when the sky is cloudless, the sun high overhead and the water unblemished by wind or roil. At such times, the tarpon below could be specimens under glass. Each anatomic feature is detailed: paired nostrils, the jet hemispheres of eyes, circles of the darkest

6

night set in the silver of a midday sky. Tarpon dorsals with their wavering lily stalk of the long, swept-back filament that is the fin's last ray; the exotic hint of violet in the scales that arch across the top of the creature's broad back; the sweeping scythe of a tail, its extended width greater than the tarpon's depth from back to belly; and the oriental coruscations of a tarpon head, an external skeleton of curving silverplate more intricate than any armor ever made for any Byzantine prince.

Yet it is the tarpon's very presence that so often obliterates such detail. For these are an ancient clan, among the oldest of all swimming species, come to this millennia from ten millennia beyond, arrived essentially unchanged from pre-history, from the earliest warm waters long before the organisms emerged from that mother sea to become the landed creatures that begot Man himself. The tarpon has outlived time and carries itself with the dignity that such vast age bestows.

It is this cloak of creation that each tarpon wears, a mantle of ancientry that no human can ever don . . . this mystery is what communicates each time one of the fish moves from behind the veil of its sea across the vision of Man. It is this mystery that transforms the weathered end of Robbie's dock into an almost holy place, a place where even corn growers, stock brokers, fashion writers, and lab assistants stand in awe of what they see at their feet. Even if they have never seen fish before, especially wild fish, swimming free, even if they are in the Keys on a trek from Duluth to escape that city's barren cold, they are as impacted when their first tarpon rolls as they would be at their entrance to the Sistine Chapel and the immortal presence of a Michelangelo.

As I watch, realizing there are no tarpon certainties when it comes to analyzing how they may take a fly, a visitor quartet begins its walk from the open-sided shed where Robbie serves his fish and chips. They have been told of the tarpon, and have ordered up three buckets of fish chunks, paid their $1.50 each, still quite unaware and totally unacquainted with what they are paying to witness.

"Oh, my God!" The rail-slim woman in her Bernardo sandals and Ralph Lauren resort shorts has just deciphered the shapes alive beneath the surface wavering beyond the dock's dark shadow.

"Come here, André, oh, come here." She calls to a middle-age man, equally slim, tan, and tailored, who carries a video camcorder. "You've never seen anything like this. There, see them. Can you get this?"

"I'll try." The man raises the camera to his shoulder, peers into the eye-piece cupped in sponge rubber. "I haven't tried shooting fish underwater before."

A tarpon rolls, its bulk rocking like a massive cradle above the surface, its lime-size scales each clearly defined in the sun's bas relief. "You can get that one," the woman exclaims, her voice pitched on discovery's adrenalin. "He's half out of the

8

water." Her arms are tight across her waist, her hands reaching for each other around her rib cage, as if they could meet at her back. She squirms in her own embrace, thrilled at the elemental grandeur of the surprise she and her friends have found in this unlikely place.

"What kind of fish are these?" she calls, the emphasis on the "are." The young, sturdy man in torn jeans and Grateful Dead T-shirt who is Robbie's manager and dockmaster answers, "Tarpon. They're tarpon," surprised that the visitor needs to ask.

In the letdown that follows the moment when the last chunk of fish has been tossed from the last bucket and the flapping pelican flock folds its hissing angular wings as the tarpon shapes subside, the woman turns to the young man. "Can you catch one for me? Can you hook one from here?"

"Why?" Her question has him off balance.

"They are so beautiful, so lovely," she says, still hugging herself and leaning out over the dock's end to keep watch. "I want to take one home with me. Have it mounted. It would be like a painting on our wall."

Shaking his head slowly, the young man says, "No." He is thinking, looking now at these lithe strangers in their meticulous vacation wardrobes, gold bracelets on thin wrists above delicately manicured nails, that what he keeps hearing about tourists is true. "No, you cannot kill these fish." He takes a breath. "The state protects them. You have to have a permit— fifty bucks—to kill one to have mounted. Just one."

He looks straight at the woman. "But I ain't killing none of these fish here"—still incredulous that anyone would ask.

Panning the horizon to the northwest and swinging to zoom in on the woman's profile, the cameraman pulls his eye back from the sponge-rubber cup, flips a switch, and lowers his camcorder, smiling. The quartet turns and heads up the dock to their waiting, coffee-colored Mercedes sedan with its blue-and-gold New York plates. I can hear their chatter as they go; the woman is still rattling with excitement over the tarpon.

Off to the northwest, where the cameraman got his closing shot, off where a collection of mangrove hammocks and small keys are scattered on Florida Bay like green leaves torn from trees tossed in a summer squall, there is a place I could find again, even though I have been there just once.

Each of those keys I can see on that distant horizon, each hammock, no matter how small, has a name, but I know none of them. This stretch of water is not my stretch. I live in Key West, more than seventy-five miles west-southwest of Robbie's dock. But there is that one day I shared a flats fishing skiff with a banker I had never met until that morning when we first shook hands at Bud & Mary's, the marina at the other, northeast, Islamorada end of the Lignum Vitae Bridge.

I was filler material for a business arrangement. It was my then Key West employer the bankers wanted, but I was invited because two flats boats had been chartered and my boss, who had known me for twenty years, understood my fishing addiction.

What he did not know, because I had never spilled the entire sloppy litany to anyone except my own tumultuous memories, was the number of times I had made contact with tarpon, only to have them end those meetings long before I wanted them gone.

September 1986: my first visit to Key West. And before midnight on that first day I had seen the first tarpon of my life and, like the woman on Robbie's dock, was swept by a desire to draw them closer, to embrace, to share the grandeur of their deliberate presence. Watching them under the lights of the Truman Annex pier, there where Gulf waters bottomed at depths of twenty feet in dredged caverns the United States Navy dug to create a safe harbor for much of its First World War submarine fleet . . . there where the great fish could visit within yards of Northwest Channel, one of their primary migratory routes, where they came in with the rising night tide to feed on shrimp and small fish the Navy's leftover lights attracted, understanding for my first time the tarpon's awesome size, comprehending some of its contained power as the fish whirled under the lights, becoming giant blades slicing as they turned and hapless shrimp vanished, I knew I wanted to live long enough to arrange a proper meeting for each of us: the great tarpon and I.

I wait, still.

Here at Robbie's I wait and watch, a mile or so from those nameless keys where the banker and I fished together on the Islamorada flats and I thought for a moment that meeting had

11

been achieved. Through the morning I had stood on the skiff's forward deck as our guide poled from his platform above the stern. Perhaps a half-dozen times tarpon glided within casting range, violet shadows whispering above pale sands, sailing like clouds on a freshening breeze through their underwater skies.

I managed, I thought, to put my fly within the ken of their consciousness, but none paid attention. We stopped, drifting through lunch, and I began again in the desperation of the shortening afternoon.

Mid-afternoon, and I sense the gentle restlessness of my banker host. His thoughts are with a cool drink on his shade-dark terrace. Mine, of a sudden, are with the two blue-velvet shapes materializing seventy feet off the bow.

"See those two?" asks the guide.

I nod, starting my back cast. The slight breeze favors me, and almost as soon as the fly lands one of the tarpon swings to take it. And does.

I strike as well as I've been taught in three years of practice and instruction. Fly line burns my palm as the fish rockets, then my rod bucks as the free line is gone and the fish is on the reel.

This is it. I dare to think that.

The fish jumps, all six feet of it, suspended there against my pounding heart.

Then it is gone.

My fly line lies dead in the water.

"I should have bowed when he jumped." I yell it, before the guide or the banker can tell me of my mistake. Because I failed to lower my rod tip as soon as the fish began his leap, the line snapped taut and the hook pulled loose.

One more for the lost list, I tell myself as we begin the trip home to Bud & Mary's.

A year, and more vanished tarpon, have gone by since. A good reason, I decide, to visit Robbie's whenever I can. Perhaps, I hope, the fish will comprehend the intensity of my yearning, may make a pact to end my quest. Hey, I tell them as I get up to leave, I'm not like that woman. I don't want to kill you and take you home. I just want a meeting. But one that ends on my terms, not yours. Then both of us can get our lives back on track.

TWO

I t's not as if other anglers have been unable to arrange proper contacts with tarpon. Indeed, rod and reel fishermen have been meeting tarpon for more than a century.

Anthony W. Dimock, the cheerful financier from the estate he called Happy Valley in Peekamoose, New York, spent as much of his time fishing as he did trying, successfully as it happened, to corner the gold market along with Jay Gould and James Fisk back in those freewheeling, robber-baron late-nineteenth-century pre-income-tax years when instant fortunes could be taken by men of ingenuity, bravado, and a gambler's willingness to risk all.

Dimock, as he reveals himself in his almost whimsical, charming, and altogether delightful volume, *The Book of the Tar-*

pon, turned each of his entrepreneurial traits to his angling advantage. Displaying a fine ingenuity, much pluck, and a daily commitment to risk his boat, his gear, and, indeed, his life in pursuit of the tarpon, he began his enduring relationship with the great fish when he became one of the first men to take one on rod and reel.

That was on a February morning in 1882 fishing from his fragile canoe with Tat, his black guide and stern man. In the mouth of Florida's Homosassa River where the current sweeps past Shell Island into the Gulf of Mexico, Dimock hooked a tarpon while he was drifting shrimp for sea trout.

When the fish leaped its first awesome leap, Dimock writes, "The brilliant rays of the semi-tropical sun made a prism of every drop in the shower that surrounded the creature. . . . At first I thought the wonderful being was a mermaid, as I noted her fierce display of activity and strength, I pitied the merman who came home late. . . . Then I suspected it was a wicked genie freed from the Seal of Solomon which had imprisoned it for thousands of years.

"I was brought back to earth by Tat: 'Mus' be a tarpum!'

"'What's that?' I asked.

"'That's what got your hook.'

"Talking in circles is profitless and I turned to my buzzing reel, shouting as I saw the diminishing line: 'Pull like smoke, Tat! Line's 'most gone.'

"Then I put on the drag, but it had no effect. I held my rod vertically and pressed my thumb hard on the reel.

"Once more the creature shot high in the air while my thumb got red hot.

"This was in February, 1882, three years before the recognition of the tarpon as a game fish. I believe the tarpon then on my line is entitled to the credit of being the first of its species captured with rod and reel."

Anthony Dimock, according to other published references, appears to be correct. Writing in his 1945 volume, *Salt Water Fishing*, Van Campen Heilner, another well-portfolioed author and sportsman, tells his readers: "Undoubtedly the first tarpon ever taken on rod and reel was taken by Mr. Samuel H. Jones of Philadelphia in March, 1884, in the Indian River Inlet, Florida. The fish weighed 172½ pounds and was taken trolling on a Buell spoon. The honor is generally supposed to have belonged to Mr. W. H. Wood who caught his fish in Surveyor's Creek, Florida, on March 25, 1885, but Mr. Jones fish antedates this by one year."

Anthony Dimock's "tarpum" antedates both by at least two years.

Both angler-authors are quick to agree, however, that each has caught more tarpon than I'll probably ever see.

Fishing the headwaters of the Encantado River in Cuba in the pre-World War Two years, Heilner and a companion hooked 105 tarpon in a single day. They were trolling spoons in a river so narrow and so overgrown that leaping tarpon often tangled their lines in the branches of riverside trees.

They were not, however, casting flies.

17

But Anthony Dimock had, a quarter-century earlier when he fished the rivers, channels, and bays of Gulf Coast Florida for a total of fifty-two days. He kept painstaking track of each one, and the grand total of tarpon taken by this one angler was 334 fish. Of those, twenty-five were caught on a fly in the Harney River; thirty-two on a fly in Turner's River; and another six in Allen's River.

A contemporary guide to fishing Florida waters advises, "Delicate split bamboo fly rods are not for the likes of tarpon . . ."

Ah, but that was all Anthony Dimock had available. His fly reels were direct drive, German silver and steel contraptions loaded with linen line controllable only by thumb pressure. He fished from a ten-foot wood-and-canvas canoe fitted with none of the stabilizing designs now taken for granted. And he and Tat capsized many times, once in the midst of hammerhead sharks drawn by the blood of a hooked tarpon one shark had halved. Dimock thought nothing of these episodes. He was so immersed in his joy of fishing that apparently he assumed no pursuit so pleasant could ever do him harm. He went after his tarpon with the same vigorous energies he expended trying to corner the gold market, and, as he would be the first to tell you, he loved the fishing more.

In the 108 years since Anthony Dimock and Tat made contact with that first "tarpum," women have been given the vote, men have been to the moon, and—when everything is working properly—both men and women who have the correct bit of plastic on their person can extract cash from vending machines, even in the middle of the night. Thus has technology accelerated in ever-increasing leaps.

In my case, however, to little or no avail. In place of Dimock's split bamboo ("not for the likes of tarpon") I possess one of the finest fly-casting rods available to contemporary anglers the world around. An example of how brilliantly the by-products of space technology can be applied to the truly important aspects of our lives, my new tarpon rod incorporates the sum total of man's knowledge of how best to take graphite and other exotic synthetics and mould them to an ultra-specialized purpose.

Fashioned expressly for me—it even has my name on it—this nine-foot rod built for a twelve-weight fly-fishing line was painstakingly created on a Loomis blank by John Graves in his shop in Glen Rose, Texas, and given to me as a gift. Why? You've got me there. Yes, John Graves is a fellow writer (a much better one) and, yes, he is and has been for many, many years married to my sister. But at no time, not for one moment, during the four decades that I have known him have I ever performed a single act of service, kindness, or even simple hard labor that warrants such a gift. Knowing well John's dedication, and knowing that no fly rod was ever built with more meticulous attention to detail, I am, of course, ever indebted. In most cases, such an obligation might prove onerous. John, however, is a gentleman of such disarming and casual grace that I have come to understand I can use the rod for all the years left me without a single twinge of conscience over the thought that I can never repay him in kind.

Ah, but if I break its tip in one of my frequent casual moments of carelessness, then what? It will be the last of me, and the last of being properly outfitted for my tarpon quest. There's no way I can ever ask my benefactor for yet another rod, and no way I can afford to replace the irreplaceable. Comparable equipment, albeit without the loving care and attention to detail, retails for $300 and up.

And worth every penny. Practicing through the long winter as I wait for the coming spring's ultimate challenge, I have discovered that high-tech does work. If I concentrate on doing everything as I know it should be done, I can toss a fly within reaching distance of first base from my stand on home plate in the empty baseball diamond where I go to rehearse. That's almost ninety feet, some twenty feet farther than last year with last year's equipment.

My Fin-Nor saltwater fly reel, also a gift—this one from Nat Reed, who, like John Graves, has never incurred, and quite likely will never incur, any such comparable benefit from me—is working flawlessly and I am casting the latest weight-forward, Tarpon-Taper line from Scientific Anglers. As you may have guessed, it is also a gift, this time from Capt. Jeffrey Cardenas, my fishing companion, guide, instructor, Key West neighbor, and friend who wants me to meet my tarpon almost as intensely as I want to meet one. Jeffrey, the 1989 "Guide of the Year" as far as *Fly Rod & Reel* magazine is concerned, is in many ways even more profligate than John and Nat. Not only has he given me my space-age fly line but he also showers me with samples of the saltwater flies he ties with such genius on the few days bad weather keeps him from putting his fortunate clients in touch with the permit, barracuda, tarpon, bonefish, and other surprises that navigate the flats west to the Marquesas and east through the back country to the Content Keys.

Jeffrey even tries to teach me the knots I should know to build my own leaders—again with materials the likes of which Anthony Dimock never imagined. What with Bimini twists, Albrights, surgeon's loops, and Homer Rhodes knots in the eighty-pound-test shock leader, it is difficult for me to remember each and every one. Thus both Jeffrey and John—also a superb fly tyer—have taken to presenting me with the total assembly: specially tied fly and fully constructed leader complete with a loop ready to be slipped on the loop already part of the leader butt that's attached to my fly line, which in turn is looped to some 250 yards of Dacron backing via a special looper for braided line lent to me by Jeffrey.

John Graves gives me flies; Nat Reed gives me flies; Jeffrey gives me flies; our children give me flies for Christmas and my birthdays; and a while ago a package arrived in the mail from a New York City banker named Howard Guja whom I took out fishing for just a few hours when he was on a short visit to Key West a year ago. I opened the wrapping and the box inside and found almost two dozen hand-tied saltwater flies of varying patterns, including two McCrab permit flies. Like John's and Nat's and Jeffrey's, they are tied on Mustad hooks, hand-sharpened to more than needle points.

In five days of fly-casting on the Harney River almost a century ago, with equipment considered less than primitive by current standards, Anthony Dimock caught twenty-five tarpon. In three years of trying in some of the best tarpon water on the planet and after being put right on top of the fish by the nation's guide of the year, I have yet to hook up with a tarpon long enough to be able to tell myself that I did everything right—well, right enough so I know it was not my mistake that allowed the escape of the very few tarpon I did encounter.

It's a good thing, I suppose, that Anthony W. Dimock is now casting over those great fishing rivers in the sky. Were he still with us in this world, he would surely be perplexed by the dimensions of my ineptitude. He'd probably send off a copy of his book inscribed "Read This. I Can Think of Nothing Else That Might Help. Where There Is Life, There Must Be Hope. AWD."

And, incredibly, there is. Although the sorry litany of my past failures runs and reruns on the bitter screen of my memory, I have not surrendered. This, I tell myself, will be the year.

I have two fishing days with Jeffrey in May. Those forty-eight hours are my finest window of opportunity. If I am guided by one of the very best there is during the week of the month when past records indicate the peak of the region's tarpon migration, and I fail yet again, I'll have only myself to blame: not my equipment, not my guide, not his equipment, and neither the season nor the venue. Only myself.

To avoid that wretched reality, I have added yet another arrow to my quiver. Thanks to the generosity and the stubborn determination of our son, Roger, there is a decent flats boat stored at the Garrison Bight Marina just down the street from our Key West home. Disregarding the inconvenience and the hazards of winter driving on snowy northeastern roads, Roger towed the sixteen-foot Grumman aluminum skiff some 2,700 miles from Maine to our doorstep, and he made the trip in record time.

After several days of recovery, he and I and John Graves (Roger and I would have been lost without John) installed the modifications that converted the boat to a fine platform for fly fishing on the flats. With a casting deck that covers the entire bow section back more than six feet and a 40-horse Evinrude that's light enough for me to handle solo when it needs to be tilted, I have, for the first time, a boat that's within ten percent of being equal to professional models.

We don't have the electric motors that some guides use these days to move toward tarpon in water too deep for poling, but I do have a set of oars in padded oarlocks, and I guarantee I can sneak up on rolling tarpon with a better chance of pulling within casting range.

In short, I have everything I need (some would say more) to get myself to where the tarpon are, stalk them, cast to them, hook one, control it, and release it on my terms—singlehanded!

Contemplating this very real possibility, I can feel my pulse stutter as my imagination zooms in on the various scenarios the encounter might assume. With determination, I can sustain such delightful daydreams for minutes on end . . . until my memory kicks in and reality takes over.

Then I'm back in the Marquesas aboard Jeffrey's *Waterlight* on the afternoon of May 24, 1988. It is the last day of two fishing days chartered by my friend Brad Burns who has flown down from Portland to try to discover why so many fellow fishermen tell him he should try tarpon on a fly. Maine born and raised, and never before in the bow of a flats boat casting to fish almost as hefty as his own 200-plus pounds, Brad, after several attempts, has hooked, landed, and released his first tarpon, a spirited fighter and classic leaper that Jeffrey estimates weighs close to a hundred pounds.

Now it's my turn, has been for the past several hours. Jeffrey locates a small school just off the Marquesas' northwest shore and the group holds long enough for him to put me in excellent casting position, no more than forty feet from the glistening backs all but lolling there on a windless sea breathing softly under a tropic sun.

I cast to the group's edge, a great shape turns and takes my fly, shocks me with its first sudden, stunning leap, then begins its run as my fly line skips and darts from the deck, yanked by the tarpon's panicked surge.

"He's on!" Jeffrey shouts.

Even as the call carries, I am coping with disaster's entrance. My rod is bent all but double. No line leaves, although my hands, wrists, and shoulders are smitten with the full force of the tarpon's lunge.

What the hell is wrong?

Before my cerebral links can transmit the message, my cry becomes academic. With a crack as loud as a rifle shot, the fly line parts. The rod is listless in my hands.

Frowning, Jeffrey calls from the stern.

I don't know how to respond. Then I decipher this particular calamity.

Because the fish was relatively close when I cast, there was perhaps twenty to thirty feet of fly line on the deck. It had to get safely through the guides before I could claim the fish was even "on the reel."

As the loops were hissing in the tarpon's wake, and because I was not guiding line properly through the cupped palm of my left hand, a loop of fly line flipped behind the rod butt, and was, split seconds later, yanked forward. But it had nowhere to go. Wedged between rod and reel seat, forced there by the weight of the big tarpon's first careening run, the line jammed

against the reel-seat edge, tightened, stretched, and parted—
Bang!

In one of those split seconds you know will live forever even as they're born, I lost fish and fly line both, along with what little remained of my pride.

I was close to tears, truly.

THREE

It's not as if tarpon are the most difficult living sea creature to hook on a fly. A poll of flats-fishing guides from Key West to Largo would put the permit at the top of that list by a twenty-to-one margin, at least. Wary from the moment they cruise from the dark, deep waters into the illuminated transparencies of the shallow flats, permit are forever on the edge of alarm; the silent shadow of a passing pelican can prompt a permit's instant exit: one flip of its sinewed, crescent tail, a flash of dull silver in the sun, and what was once a presence has instantly become a memory, and a blurred one at that.

Not so the tarpon. Especially in the warming days of a late spring on its way toward summer. With their minds more on sex than safety, groups of shoal-water tarpon can be approached

with the expectation that if that approach is silent, soft, and skilled, the fish will hold their ground, at least until even a mediocre fly-caster (such as I) can lob the orange and yellow feathers of a Stu Apte Special close enough to catch a tarpon's eye. Whether they will leave their courting for a swipe at what must be a micro-morsel for a one-hundred-pound dynamo is another question. But enough of them do to make fishing for them a reasonable endeavor for rational anglers. (The irrationality of those who pursue the permit, however, is well known in the fly-fishing fraternity.)

In the first seventy-five days of 1990, for example, anglers guided by Captain Jeffrey Cardenas aboard his *Waterlight* hooked and released twenty-four tarpon. Dozens more were "jumped": hooked and then broken off by anglers who wanted the thrill of the contact but also wanted to spare themselves and the fish the trauma of a long and exhausting battle. And on one benign Sunday of solicitous southerly breezes—his so-called day off—Jeffrey took himself on a fishing trip and hooked, fought, landed, and released a ninety-pound tarpon on a fly. Adding that achievement to the *Waterlight*'s total, the captain's tarpon average is one fish every three days. If you deduct the number of fishing trips scrubbed by high winds and rain (yes, despite what the travel folders promise, Key West winters have their times of tumult and bluster) that average approaches a successful tarpon encounter every other fishing day.

At that rate, at this point in the afternoon of my angling

years, I should have hooked and landed at least fifteen; I've spent at least thirty long and determined days trying, not to mention various half-days and spur-of-the-moment dawn expeditions, hoping that by the time the office opened, I'd be back with a tarpon memory to sustain me.

Ah well, as I have promised, this will be the year. Instead of being envious of Jeffrey's happy anglers, I should be encouraged by their impressive successes. There are, however, also sturdy reasons why I continue harboring a thought that is requiring more and more living space in my consciousness: what if I am destined never to hook and release a tarpon, never to know beyond doubt that I am enough of a fly fisherman to maintain a kind of control over just one of these ancient and spirited beings. What then? Am I cursed, like some waterborne Quixote, to roam these southern seas tilting at windmills of the morning on a quest without end?

There are times when I can answer yes, and do it with conviction.

Take January 8, 1990, for example.

The day was a gift: one of those seasonal surprises that are bestowed only in these southernmost U.S. latitudes. Under a cloudless sky with temperatures striding confidently toward 85 degrees Fahrenheit, the *Waterlight* left Garrison Bight with me aboard, the guest of a man who had chartered Jeffrey for the entire week. The angler was Mark Rosenburg, a movie producer who had a hit on his hands. Not only a hit, but Mark's

Fabulous Baker Boys starred, among others, Michelle Pfeiffer, who became one of the year's five Academy Award nominees for "best actress."

A jolly fisherman who might have cast himself as the lead in *The Young Santa Claus*, Mark, like so many successful young professionals, had set out to learn to become a fly fisherman. And, as Jeffrey poled his skiff along a small channel northwest of Boca Grande Key, Mark stood solid on the bow's casting platform, his fly rod ready with a tarpon fly. Few, if any, tarpon had been seen, but Jeffrey believed the day's soft southerlies and the recent—and aberrant—stretch of warm weather had nudged water temperatures into the fish's comfort range.

He said as much, and the tarpon proved him correct within minutes after we had begun our channel drift. Like Neptune's engines on a secret mission, tarpon backs and shoulders rose shyly here and there among eddies of a freshening flood tide. We drifted into their midst and before he could properly savor the awesome impact of this momentous meeting, Mark was hearing Jeffrey call, "Cast now. Cast now. Now strip, slower. That's it, now strip again."

As I watched the first-timer from Hollywood do the best he could to follow his guide's direction, I told myself: "If he hooks one, I will say nothing, nothing whatsoever. No whining about beginner's luck, no recitation of my sorry history. 'Congratulations, Mark!' That's all he'll hear from me."

From my perch on the rear deck below Jeffrey's poling plat-

30

form, I saw several shadows about thirty feet off the boat's bow, dark shapes as familiar and mysterious as childhood memories. Moving as easily as thoughts through time in the airy water, the tarpon trio came closer.

"Cast now!" Jeffrey called and Mark responded. His fly dimpled the channel about thirty feet from the bow and sank slowly within the shadows' ken. "Strip, strip," said Jeffrey, his words a metronome that timed Mark's slow retrieve.

In the underwater world of my focus, a silent silver explosion detonated as one of the great tarpon rolled on its side, struck the fly, and turned Mark to stone. Witnessing a tarpon's awesome bulk at such close range and for the first time had, as it had so often for me, undone the angler's response. Just as I have done countless times, Mark stood stock still, watching the pageant unfold, forgetting that he himself was on stage and cast as co-star.

In micro-seconds, the tarpon dropped the fly and spun, the turbulence of its turning opening writhing petals on the glassy surface.

"He's gone," Jeffrey said softly. "Well, let's find another."

And he did, but none within Mark's casting range. As the day matured to mid-morning, the tarpon vanished in that undersea vastness where fish disappear as silently as stars at dawn. It was after they had gone that I was invited to take a turn on the bow. To no avail, as it happened. Other than demonstrating to myself and Jeffrey the margin of improvement in my casting, my tarpon time on that splendid day was little more than a rehearsal for a role I'd already played. And in spite of telling myself I shouldn't allow it, an insistent voice from within kept saying that if I'd been casting instead of Mark, I would not have missed that fish.

There are, after all, times when selfish arrogance may be called for.

Over the next six weeks, Jeffrey made a point of his tarpon silences. He knew my quest and wanted to avoid aggravating my yearnings with more reports of his successes. But I pressed for details, relentlessly.

I learned, for example, that on January 24 Jeffrey's charter—a fly-fisher in my age bracket, casting flies Jeffrey had tied—caught and released a one-hundred-pound tarpon, a fifteen-pound permit, and two barracuda that each weighed in at more than twenty-five pounds. All that in one of the year's shorter days, and on the day after another of Jeffrey's charters jumped a 150-pound tarpon.

One more, then I'll quit. Just a few minutes after sunrise on February 21, the *Waterlight* came to a gliding stop in a small channel near Boca Grande Key. Its lone passenger stood and walked to the bow where she began unlimbering a fly rod rigged for tarpon. If she was nervous about this initial test of her prowess as a saltwater fly fisher, she didn't show it. As Jeffrey climbed to the stern poling platform, the angler began stripping line from the reel, letting it fall in loose coils on the deck.

Intent on keeping the line tidy, trying to avoid the possibility of tangles, she never saw the tarpon that rolled thirty feet off the bow. Jeffrey did.

"Cast!" he called. "Cast to eleven o'clock. They're right in front of us! There! Right there!"

Raising her rod, the angler made one false cast, then dropped the fly about twelve feet in front of the boat. Not yet accustomed to retrieval techniques, she simply stood there while the fly sank slowly.

Within three seconds, the waters erupted. Practically at the angler's feet, a great tarpon's wash tub of a mouth engulfed the fly as the fish simultaneously turned to avoid colliding with the *Waterlight*. As the turn's arc tightened and the tarpon's head swung away from the bow, the fly pulled toward the near corner of its still-open mouth.

On the fourth second the fish had hooked itself solidly at the hinge of its jaws, the precise spot where a hook has the best odds of staying where it is.

At the fifth second, sensing the barb for the first time, the tarpon leapt clear, its almost structural bulk hung against the orange eastern sky, a living missile fired from an untamed undersea armory.

The splash as the fish careened from air back to sea tossed foam on the *Waterlight*'s deck, soaked the angler's shirt.

As the sixth second blended with the seventh and the tarpon began its hurtling run toward the Gulf's deeper waters, line hissed from the deck and then the reel. Reflexively, the angler moved to slow the shrilling reel, tried to grab the spinning handles with her hand. By the eighth second, she screamed as blood dripped from severely skinned knuckles and the tarpon's run continued.

Through the drama's first ten seconds, Jeffrey's heart was so high in his throat he could not speak. About the time the first run slowed, the guide found his voice and first-aid kit.

Incredibly, the tarpon could not shake free. Once a semblance of order was restored, the angler proved her grit, kept at her work and, with Jeffrey's calm instructions delivered every few moments, she began to draw even with her fish.

Within ninety minutes, she had her first tarpon on a fly alongside the *Waterlight* where Jeffrey measured its length and girth and then released it in good shape. It was, the captain estimated, about an eighty-pound fish.

One cast—and a twelve-footer at that—one trophy, in the very first hour of the very first day the angler had ever tossed a fly at a tarpon.

There now! How is a fellow expected to react to that sort of news from the flats? Does it mean, on the one hand, that my tarpon quest is more achievable than it appears? Or is it one more thread in the fabric of the angler's curse that has fallen on my shoulders like a shroud. I have some knowledge of these things. Salmon eluded me for four years while all around me others flaunted theirs.

When a first-time caster hooks and then lands a tarpon on her first time out, that establishes, in my mind at least, that if your stars are in harmony, superlative skills are not required. Currently, I know and Jeffrey knows that my fly-casting and fish-fighting proficiencies are, at the very least, adequate. On certain good days, I would rate them somewhat better, say perhaps a six or a seven on a scale of one to ten. And yet, and yet, after three years I am tarponless. And along comes a visitor who, on a scale of one to ten is barely a one, and she leaves Key West after two days on the flats with her tarpon measured at the *Waterlight*'s side.

Thinking about this burden, I have decided it's not that heavy. I mean, at my age—now sixty-seven—courting a modest obsession is not necessarily a negative. On given days, I do, in fact, swing full circle and can almost make myself believe it is my good fortune that tarpon have so convincingly eluded me on so many occasions.

What, I ask myself, will I have to look forward to when and if this quest is resolved in my favor? Here in South Florida the landscape is littered with my contemporaries living their so-called golden years in a kind of resigned haze. They wait for Godot and that, in and of itself, becomes a way of life.

While I, on the other hand, endlessly court financial ruin merely by traveling to tarpon country each winter. Unlike a great many more prudent folks of all ages, I am constantly living either on the monetary edge, or I am free-falling off the brink headed for penury's dark chasms. Tarpon have me trying to maintain two distant households when one is more than I can handle.

So perhaps this should be the year. My creditors will doubtless agree. And yet, once that great silver creature is there beneath my hand, to be set free at my command, a long chapter in my book of life will end. What then, I wonder?

There will be, I'm almost certain, no fish to take its place. More than a century ago, that other tarpon-quester, Anthony W. Dimock (would that I had been *his* heir) was decidedly unequivocal in his choice of the planet's number-one game fish.

"To one who has known the tarpon," he wrote, "the feeble efforts of the salmon to live up to its reputation are saddening. . . . Time would be wasted in seeking for comparison among lesser fish than salmon, and a fish that doesn't jump when played is quite out of the tarpon's class. Thus the horse mackerel, despite his being the fad of the California coast, will have to practice aviation before his picture can be placed in the Piscatorial Hall of Fame. . . . The tarpon meets every demand the sport of fishing can make. He fits the light fly rod as no trout ever dreamed of doing and leaps high out of the water a hundred times for every once that a brook trout clears the surface. When grown the size of an average man, a tarpon is no less active, although he will snap a line of thirty threads and break a hickory hoe handle as you or I would break a reed."

Go for it, Tony. Every word I consume that reinforces this creature's immortal force is salve for an aching psyche. And yet,

36

the tarpon is no myth, and as I have been so often told, it is foolish to endow any creature with what amounts to super-human qualities. Nature is, after all, fact and not fancy.

If that is true, and I'm still not 100 percent certain, then what are the tarpon data: the sort of stuff biologists and engineers and computer programmers would want to know, as opposed to my notions of a monumental silver obsession launched from the sea's unknowable chasms to haunt my senior years.

FOUR

A s I read the tarpon literature, most of it the work of dedicated researchers, I learn first that even though their scientist/authors turn out astringent academic papers, they are fascinated by the creature. And why not? It is, as Richard A. Wade, a former executive director of the American Fisheries Society in Washington and marine biologist at the University of Miami's Institute of Marine Science, has written, "an ancient and honored fish surviving from another geological epoch. Few such bony fishes have so old an ancestry."

There is more romance than research in those words, and until the twentieth century had passed its halfway mark, romance and fable were well mixed with the few scientific papers available to those who wanted an accurate compendium of tarpon data: life history, spawning habits, range, metabolism, respiration, diet, migrations, anatomy, and more. Serious efforts to compile well-substantiated tarpon facts have never had much momentum. Some studies were done through each of the decades starting with the 1900s, and all but a very few were initiated in Florida, modestly funded and researched by men and women who put in long hours on the water and in their laboratories.

For although the tarpon is a food fish in some Latin American and African nations, it is not a consumer item in United States fish markets. It is a game fish, and a rather exotic one at that. When it comes to funding research grants, both the government and most private sources are most interested in those projects that affect the most people and involve the most money. Much more, for example, is known about the sardine and the cod than about the tarpon and the bonefish—who are related, by the way, and never show up in cans or boxes at the supermarket.

There are some thirty orders of what ichthyologists label "the true bony fishes." Of these, the tarpon is the most primitive (scientifically speaking, based on its skull structure and its caudal skeleton) of this superorder Teleosti. The great silver fish that ranges the entire South Atlantic and Caribbean coasts is one of the suborder Elopoidei and the family Megalopidae. Of the single genus *Megalops*, the species that I have been chasing for three years is the Atlantic tarpon, *megalops atlanticus*, which translates roughly to "large-headed resident of the ocean edges." That, in my opinion, is pretty good nomenclature for a scientist to generate.

Following World War Two, sportsfishermen began nudging *Megalops* higher on the research priority list. For it was during the 1950s that the conflict began to pay dividends in the form of rods, reels, and lines that had not been imagined twenty years earlier. Nylon, Dacron, monofilaments, plastics, and molded-glass fibers put excellent fishing tackle within range of the most modest budgets, and general prosperity did the rest. Almost anyone who wanted to get on the water could, with the help of time payments, mass-produced boats that were also seaworthy, and a new generation of dependable and affordable inboard and outboard power plants. The days when you needed to be a banker or broker or railroad baron to be able to plan a Florida fishing trip were gone forever.

And it was the tarpon that thrilled so many of those newly arrived anglers. From Aransas, Texas, along the entire Gulf and the Florida panhandle, down the west coast from Dimock's first favorite, the Homosassa, from Boca Grande Pass, the waters off Fort Myers, and from there south past the Everglades to the Keys: Largo, Marathon, Islamorada, and from Key West southwest to Mule Key, Seven Sisters, Man Key, Woman Key, and across the channel where the Gulf meets the Atlantic to the Marquesas . . . everywhere there were tarpon, from Florida to Mexico to Central America and south below the equator.

But it was Florida that was the angling epicenter. As more and more of an increasingly mobile and outdoor America discovered that these tough, lovely, large, and dramatic fighters could be taken on everything from hooks baited with mullet chunks or crabs or shrimp, to bait-casting plugs, trolling spoons, or saltwater flies, a multi-million-dollar business began to build around a fish that seemed designed to give sports fishermen everything they had ever dreamed a fish could give. Caught from piers and bridges, from rowboats, canoes, and inflatables, as well as flats skiffs, charter boats, and power craft of every size, the tarpon sparked what amounted to a full-scale recreational industry.

And that's when interest in tarpon research began to gather enough momentum to attract significant state, federal, and private funding, albeit modest by any measure. Those were not hook-and-release days, even though Anthony Dimock, three-quarters of a century earlier, had written: "Don't murder your fish. Why slay these beautiful, harmless creatures that have contributed so much to your pleasure. It is not only cruel, but unfair to your fellow sportsmen." He was well ahead of his time.

For as interest in recreational fishing exploded, the business of mounting fish also boomed. Successful anglers wanted that permanent evidence of their supremacy hanging over their trophy-room mantel. In those times, there was little or no computerized, replica plaster-cast taxidermy—today's technique that builds a replicate trophy from measurements taken just before the tarpon is released. And many charter and flats skiff skippers encouraged anglers to bring their day's catch back to the dock for photographs. Sportfishing books and periodicals of the era are filled with the classic victory pose: dead fish in a row hanging from an overhead beam, the fisherman and guide on either side wearing triumphant smiles. No one considered the rightness or wrongness of the tradition; everybody—Hemingway included—did it, and that was that.

There was no accurate count of the Florida tarpon kill, and no way to get one. Several hundred fish might be taken in a single May week from just one good-size charter-boat dock. Brought back in the evening, tarpon carcasses would be hauled out to sea the next morning and left for the sharks. But a handful of Florida's young marine biologists—scientists on the leading edge of the developing environmental and ecological sensitivities that would later become national policy—began to ask questions. What did anyone know, if anything, about the tarpon population? Could it sustain a growing annual mortality rate? And, more importantly, what if the tarpon kill combined with the loss of tarpon breeding grounds to generate a population crash?

Which led, in turn, to the initial focus of the first significant tarpon research: Where and how do tarpon spawn and what are the nursery environments for juvenile fish? A part of this question still waits to be answered thirty years later. To accurately locate tarpon spawning grounds, researchers need to recover recently released tarpon eggs, preferably just hours old. To date, no such eggs have been discovered.

Ah, but the researchers get closer each year. And, like my quest, theirs may also be fulfilled soon. During June and July, Roy E. Crabtree and his crew from the Florida Marine Research Institute will be cruising both Florida coasts aboard research vessels outfitted with specialized towing gear designed to collect minute marine organisms. The effort, primarily federally funded, but also aided by state and private support (in this case the Hawley Foundation) is a continuation of a hunt Roy Crabtree has pursued for several years.

As a result of these efforts, the Institute already has what is very likely the largest collection of premetamorphic tarpon larvae in the world: more than 260 larvae, some less than a quarter-inch long and showing traces of their egg's yolk still attached. Which means those tiniest tarpon were born a few days before they were collected in late June about one hundred miles off Florida's west coast.

If you could look at one of these creatures under a microscope expecting to see a miniature tarpon, you would not only be surprised, but perhaps even frightened. For what is known as the tarpon's leptocephalus stage (see illustration) could, if it grew to more than two hundred pounds, become a dragon as terrifying as any from China's mythology or those slain by the knights of Edmund Spenser's *The Faerie Queen*. Dagger teeth

44

protrude from jaws that occupy much of the grotesque head with its great, black eyes. Yet the long, ribbonlike body that stretches from this toothy head could belong to a ceremonial dragon paraded through the streets of Beijing on a Chinese New Year. With its digestive tract, spinal structure, and even its brain visible in the translucent flesh that ends in a strangely floral tail, the organism that will become a juvenile tarpon within a few months appears to bear no relation to the sleek and powerful creature many anglers call the silver king.

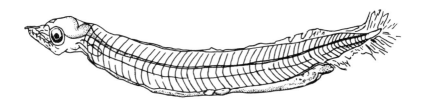

The metamorphosis from what must be one of the uglier ducklings in the ichthyological world (eels, bonefish, lady fish, and spiny eels share related transformations) takes somewhere between six and eight weeks. In the process, the tiny dragons grow to about an inch-and-a-half; then, as they transform, like Charles Hyde back to Dr. Jekyll, they begin to grow smaller. "The fish that grows by shrinking . . ." is how one researcher describes this complex transformation. What emerges, in three months or so, is the true juvenile tarpon: a fish that looks like a fish, even though it's less than an inch long.

Its dorsal fin is already prominent; even the final ray that will grow to become the long, stalky fin is in place. Those bony gill plates that will rattle when the adult tarpon leaps are also well defined; the large eyes are in their proper place and the curving crescent of the powerful tail has begun to take shape. Not much longer than a postage stamp, this is, however, definitely an infant fish. Unlike the dragon that it was just a few weeks before, it is a creature you would, if you had ever seen its adult forebears, quickly be able to identify as a tarpon, albeit one so fragile you might fear for its survival.

And well you should. For it is at this stage of its life that the tarpon as a proper fish (as opposed to either an egg or a lectocephalus larvae) is in greatest danger from scores of predators, both finned and winged. As protection, the juveniles look for small backwaters, tidal ponds that may open to the sea once or twice a year during hurricanes or extraordinary tides, drainage ditches accessible only through culverts, small coves back in the mangroves where the water is so rich in organic material that it looks more like black-bean soup than gin. All the better to hide in, the juveniles will tell you.

Those that make it—and although researchers have learned a mature tarpon female (140 pounds) lays more than twelve million eggs, they have no accurate data on survival ratios—grow quickly. Adapting to salinities that range from fresh to brackish to salt and feeding on a diet that includes plenty of mosquito larvae, the juveniles grow to adolescents more than a foot long in less than ten months. A year later, they have evolved into miniatures of the fierce game fish they will become and a host of Florida fly fishermen have learned that casting small bonefish flies in the most unlikely places—from atop culverts and into golf-course water hazards—can produce three-to-ten-pound tarpon that are not only eager eaters but leap and battle as dramatically and bravely as their parents.

I have plans for some of these young bucks. A Key West fisherman, Ed Little, Jr., who not only presides at the National Marine Fisheries office in the city's Federal Building but also works as a marine fisheries consultant and who was the driver on Mel Fisher's crew who helped pinpoint the *Atocha*'s treasure, is a compulsive angler/explorer. Even on his infrequent holidays, he takes the time and, more importantly, makes the effort to locate new fishing treasures. Those efforts have included wading through hip-deep muck, squirming around and through mangrove tangles, and hauling small inflatable boats across barriers that thwart egrets and herons—all this in angling's name. As the beneficiary of Ed Little's determination, I have been promised an expedition to one of those small, hidden, brackish backwaters that acts as a kind of junior high school for young tarpon in transition. Perhaps, I tell myself, if the grownups continue to defeat me in the Gulf and the Atlantic, then their children (with Ed Little's help) will not be so

47

lucky. And even though it may weigh in at less than five pounds, I may still have my tarpon on a fly.

Like Roy Crabtree and his associates, and like Richard Wade and his legion of scientist counterparts, Ed Little wants to learn as much about tarpon as there is to learn. I cannot, in truth, say the same. For while I have probed with some energy and persistence much of the body of tarpon knowledge that exists, this research is not a lifetime commitment. It's quite likely that once the great fish and I have settled our score, I'll move along, leaving further tarpon data and tarpon lore to the Littles and Crabtrees of the marine research establishment.

Which is not to say that I haven't been fascinated by much of what I've discovered with their help. Indeed, once you have gathered even a few rudimentary facts about the tarpon, you become quite certain that it is a *bona fide* anomaly of the seas, so different in so many significant ways from the creatures most of us visualize when we hear "fish" that it deserves another label, one quite its own.

It is, for one, a fish that breathes, and not merely by absorbing oxygen from the water it filters with its feathered, crimson gills. No. For the tarpon, gills are not enough. This fish has what's been called a "lung-like internal swim bladder." I am still uncertain why just plain "lung" is not a fitting and accurate definition for a biological membrane rich in capillaries able to extract oxygen from inhaled air. Which is how the tarpon is so uniquely equipped.

They sigh. I have heard them. Drifting in Northwest Channel with our engines shut down, watching for any signal that tarpon might be sliding beneath us in their secret depths, I have heard the great fish before I've seen them. And I have come to understand how those first sailors, those awesomely determined and courageous men who set sail in fragile craft on unknown seas, could build their belief in mermaids. For often when a tarpon first rolls the silver pillar of its massive back above a still and windless surface, its exhalation from that tarpon lung is a sibilant sigh, a mournful release quite unlike any other sound heard at sea, so laden with an immortal sadness.

We have, Jeffrey and I, often trailed tarpon bubbles that rise like a diver's when the fish empties its lung as it swims submerged. And as a tarpon battles for its life at the end of a line, this breathing becomes labored like a runner's at the finish of a punishing race. There is, in its human rhythms, an invitation to anthropomorphize this creature. A fish that struggles so to breathe as it senses its life is in peril alongside your boat is a fish that stabs the conscience of your soul.

But this, the marine biologists will explain, is not the lung's biological function. That, they will say, is still not fully understood, although available evidence and research results indicate it does enable the fish to range from salt to fresh to brackish and even soupy water, just as it also gives the tarpon an additional oxygen supply, a kind of booster power for the incredible engine that generates such wonderous propulsion. One fact has been established: tarpon must rise to inhale air. The frequency and rhythm of its breathing may vary, but it is essential to the creature's life. This was proven to scientific satisfaction when a dozen tarpon were sealed in a glass-topped tank completely filled with water. Even though the water was generously aerated, all the tarpon died within a few days.

That supercharged metabolic system that powers the tarpon may also be the reason the fish is such an accomplished and exuberant leaper. I like to think that tarpon, like each of us, know those mornings when the world's wonder cannot be ignored. Full of enthusiasm for life itself, the tarpon leaps—just for the fun of it. That, too, I have seen. As we drifted near Seven Sisters, waiting for dawn to become day, a tarpon rocketed from beneath the channel, its full six-foot silver mass rose and rose until its tail cleared the surface by at least two feet, then, for a timeless moment, that shape of the living morning hung there, turned a bit on its side, fell back with a broad blossoming of spray and white foam, and was gone.

"How I love to see that," Jeffrey said.

Measured, again by scientists, tarpon leaps have been recorded at vertical heights of more than ten feet; swimming at top speed and leaping more horizontally, like porpoises, tarpon have been airborne for a measured twenty feet.

A huge fish that breathes and flies! No wonder the tarpon has become part of the littoral mythology from temperate zone to temperate zone both north and south of the Atlantic equator. A creature known to every Atlantic coastal culture, it ranges over an incredible 80 degrees of latitude and east from the Caribbean and South America to the shores of Africa's Dakar and the Belgian Congo. Called "caffum" in the Barbados, the *grande ecaille* by Cajuns, the *grande ecoy* in East Texas, "silver fish" in Pensacola, "big scale" in Massachusetts, and *sabalo, sadina, savalo, savalle,* and *savanilla* by Hispanic peoples, the tarpon's most popular North American colloquial name is "tarpum," descended from the American Indians and first used in the creature's sporting literature by Tat, Anthony Dimock's guide.

Sustained by the folklore that grew in the wake of its impressive presence, the tarpon itself helped spawn some of the mystery and misinformation that has encouraged much of the current interest among marine researchers. Today's biologists are skeptical of most early studies, and some recently acquired data prove their point. Two decades ago, the scientific community generally agreed that almost all tarpon lived out their lives within twenty years. Current investigations, reported by Roy Crabtree, tell us that tarpon are much longer lived. "They reach ages in excess of forty-five years," the marine biologist writes. "Females attain larger size than males, and almost all fish of more than one hundred pounds are females. Sexual maturity probably occurs at an age of around seven-to-ten years and a size of about sixty pounds for females. Males mature at a smaller size—perhaps forty pounds—and probably a younger age." However, like the good researcher that he is, Roy

Crabtree qualifies each of his conclusions. "Most of our results," he explains, "are still preliminary and I am hesitant to make too much of them. It is much easier to say, 'I don't know' than to make a statement and then discover I was wrong. However, having said that, I am confident that our conclusions about longevity and size will hold up to later scrutiny."

It enlightens me somewhat to learn who the tarpon players are in terms of size and sexual maturity. At least the next time I witness what I am convinced is a kind of tarpon courtship ballet, I may be able to identify just which of them is dancing the male and female roles.

For we see these ballets often in the Marquesas, Jeffrey and I. "Daisy chaining" is how guides describe the exotic assembly: a schooling of these great fish in shoal water, usually no more than six or ten feet deep. The gathering is circular, an almost formal display that is a kind of set piece, as rigidly prescribed as a classic *pas de deux*. All but ignoring our skiff, as many as twenty or thirty tarpon turn on a kind of submerged carousel, around and around in a circle no more than sixty feet across.

Accompanied by the ethereal sounds of their sighing, the troupe swims on the surface, a gathering of gleaming giants, first their coruscated heads emblazoned with that vast jet jewel of an eye, then the blue-violet shoulders followed by the cool blaze of silver torsos, and finally the scimitar tails slicing the Gulf as the tarpon submerge only to surface again in moments to repeat the same, slow, graceful patterns, around and around and around, a mysterious living galaxy orbiting in its silent space on a mission we cannot comprehend.

A fish that breathes, flies . . . and dances! Given the scheduling of this pageant in May and June—the very months when data indicate the tarpon spawns—I am convinced the daisy chain ballets are a courtship ritual, the ritual that begins the mystery that produces that still-secret fertilized egg that becomes the tiny dragon of the depths. And it is that dragon that transforms to a still smaller tarpon that can survive to live almost half a century on a diet as eclectic as crabs, water ticks, insects, mullet, graylings, anchovies, sheat-fish, silversides, pinfish, catfish, and shrimp, and grow to more than eight feet and weigh in at 350 pounds like the great tarpon netted off Florida's Hillsboro Inlet decades ago.

There are, I'm sure, more tarpon like that one. Able in most cases to outswim its only natural enemies—the dolphin and the shark—tarpon are proven survivors, as millennia testify. The one force they have not adapted to is Man: still eminently capable of not only the tarpon's destruction, but also the slaughter of every organism caught in the path of development, pesticides, pollution, abused habitat, and resource exploitation.

In Florida, in the tarpon's case, a newly energized combining of resource conservation and research is now well under way. Tarpon can no longer be heedlessly caught and killed. With a single exception, all hooked tarpon must be released; if a licensed angler wants to keep one trophy fish for mounting, he must have a Florida permit to do so, and it will cost him $50.

Given these enlightened policies and the discoveries Roy Crabtree and his contemporaries are making and will continue to report, there is no possibility, I am quite certain, that the tarpon will vanish before I do. Like Tat and Anthony Dimock, Captain Jeffrey and I will pursue our tarpum quest, secure that these wondrous creatures wait for us, there in the warm seas that are their world, and have been for far longer than this one has been ours.

FIVE

Like so many missions, our tarpon voyages have led us to unexpected adventures, unforeseen discoveries, and even a few unexpected conquests. Just as their first look at the Snake River must have dazzled Meriwether Lewis and William Clark as much, or more, than their eventual arrival at the Pacific Coast, Jeffrey and I have been thrilled by totally unanticipated encounters on the flats. Like a gold coin flashing in the fingers of the magician who has snatched it from the very air, the wild treasures that materialize from beneath the flat's dancing waters are stunning in their suddenness.

It is this dimension for drama, this capacity for revelation that endows the flats with their unique mystery and attraction. Offshore, where waters run deep, a surfacing fish is surely a welcome and breathtaking sight. But out there, where the sea shields its soul, only the creatures who surface are seen. On the flats, where thin water is a window on an entire submerged universe, an observant drifter standing tall on the deck of a silent boat can witness an entire range of undersea comings and goings by a teeming variety of wild beings.

And when the brilliant south Florida sun is overhead, pummeling a windless surface with its intense illumination, and boat and boat people keep their presence properly discreet, the underwater communities of the thin water can be observed at peace with their environment, doing what they do in the privacy of what is most often their own secret world. We are, Jeffrey and I, adrift on the *Waterlight*, often more intimately introduced to the daily dramas of this free, wild place than even a diver is. Watching from above, often we can see without being seen. Any submerged presence, even a diver motionless in the shadow of a coral head, is too much of an alien being to enter undetected. Fish will swim close to a diver, even nuzzle the suited shape. But because that shape is instantly documented as abnormal, every sea creature's behavior is somehow modified to deal with the new arrival.

From below, the slim hull of the drifting *Waterlight* could be one more bit of the flotsam that meanders the currents of these tropical seas. Hatch covers, palm fronds, uprooted trees—whatever the detritus of man and nature that makes its way to water becomes a part of this world, not its invader. If we are motionless on deck, part of the inanimate structure and not living passengers aboard it, we can often become invisible voyeurs, able to witness the savage innocence of the wonderfully wild creatures of the flats. Until we raise an arm, lift a fly rod, take a step along the deck, set down a thermos, or crunch the push pole into the marly bottom, we can glide beyond the veil that so often separates beings above water from those below.

So a day when no fish are "caught" is not a day when no fish are seen. This seeing is a bonus more flats anglers must learn to recognize. And it is a key element in the transition every angler senses in these times of movement from the days when fishing meant killing to a future when fishing will mean meeting. Yes, hooking up can still be the pivotal purpose of a day on the flats. It is, after all, the ultimate test of how well a fly-caster has mastered his skills and how well a flats guide has learned his trade. But while the hook-up hunt is in progress, there is more to be found on the flats than signs of quarry. Often I find the myriad dramas so diverting that my fishing, my casting, and hooking is forgotten, and I spend more time watching a leopard ray's magnificent and rippling span than I do looking for a tarpon's pearly roll.

I have a rod ready, of course. But more and more I find I am content to watch, to sweep the flats as diligently as any masthead lookout sent aloft by Captain Ahab to sight the white whale. Because there is so much to see. To see and to remember. A single silver mullet still dances in my vision, recalled to my internal screen whenever my thoughts become waterborne, as they so often do. The fish appeared off our stern, shot from the sea by the explosion of its own terror. Its first leap was close to flight, a solo soaring arc that ended in a white foamburst six feet off our starboard rail. The small blossom of its re-entry became, in a split second, the launch site of the mullet's next leap, a silver curve almost as dramatic as the first that carried the scaled projectile beyond our bow where it once again took to the air as the compact energy of its panic endowed the foot-long mullet with a kind of superfish ability to fly faster than a speeding bullet.

Sensing rather than seeing a secondary disturbance in the space the mullet just vacated, I looked back to the flats to our starboard and saw the dark green and silver shape of a four-foot barracuda charging past. If the concentrated energies of the mullet's panic were awesome, the raw force of the cuda's charge was breathtaking. No cuda at the end of my fly line had ever moved with such accelerating power. Doomed, I thought, that mullet is doomed. But its diminishing splashes ended at a mangrove fringe bordering a small hammock. There the foot-deep water boiled with the barracuda's turnings as it patroled the mangrove picket line, waiting for the mullet to make its last mistake.

There are few beginnings and endings to these one-act flats dramas. Jeffrey and I seldom, if ever, see these wild interactions develop, accelerate, and conclude. Instead, we witness a part of the action, the sudden flowering of a silver bouquet as two dozen ballyhoo leap simultaneously in a living fountain of escape from predators whose shadows dance across the white marl bottom like dark scarves in a gale.

In a channel that meanders across the flats from the Gulf to the Atlantic, a bluer artery pumping life from one sea to the other, a nurse shark, perhaps half as long as the *Waterlight* and infinitely more terrible, glides within two feet of our bow, cruising the channel's coral demarcation, the steep incline that marks the flats' end and beginning, the underwater riverbank that holds the channel's surging currents in place, giving a shark this large the vitality it needs to survive the closeness of such a relatively small space. If the shark is aware that I stand less than two feet above, able if I chose to jump squarely astride the thick back writhing, it does not tell me. As primitive as a redwood's massive root, the shark eases its sinuous bulk carefully, as if enemies, or perhaps prey, might be discovered at any moment on what appears from above to be a rather languid and menacing stroll. Before any change in this remarkable pace, the shark glides further, then vanishes in the channel's distant dark, more impressive now that I know it's there, but invisible.

We are not always so fortunate, Jeffrey and I. More times than not, we discount a sea creature's abilities to sense our presence. Then we get sudden exits instead of one-minute dramas. Water boils, its convulsions duplicating the thrust of a great tarpon tail, the push of a shark's torso, or the shove of a ray's wings against a cloud of marl stirred from the bottom by the silent gale of a great ray's flight. Barracuda are less inclined to hasty departures. They may dart away, but often they return. Their curiosity gets the best of them and they cruise alongside, parallel visitors, their heads cocked a bit, their black boatside eye looking directly at me as I stand on the bow returning their stare.

To me, barracuda are the most intelligent fish on the flats. Unlike their brethren, they seem to have reached a kind of understanding with humans: they are quite certain they know who we are and, more times than not, they are not about to be deceived by a fly twitched past their long and pointed noses. But, like humans, they are not infallible. Now and then, propelled by curiosity, hunger, and perhaps a sense of mischief, cuda attack a fly as if it threatened their children. Their rush is startling and often so frenzied that the cuda misses its strike. Sometimes it will make a second or a third irritated lunge. I like these encounters. Often the fish follows the fly to the boat and we make eye contact: the cuda looking up, me down, both of us highly entertained.

All fish that visit the flats are cautious about being discovered too far from an accessible escape. Flats along the edges of relatively deep channels are most likely to be popular with hefty oceanic visitors: sharks, rays, big barracuda, tarpon, permit, and bonefish. A few miles southwest of Key West, between Crawfish Key on the east and Man Key to the west, a series of channels slices across the broad flats that divide the Atlantic from the Gulf. There are seven of them and guides know the place as the Seven Sisters.

Of the waters, lagoons, reefs, flats, hammocks, and islands within a thirty-minute boat ride from Key West's littered harbor—and there is a wealth of mystery within that thirty-minute circle—the Seven Sisters is one of my favorites. It is a magnificent concurrence of shallows and depths, Gulf and Atlantic, flats and channels. Running east and west, the ribbon of flats stretching from Crawfish Key to Man Key can be approached from the Gulf side on the north where a natural basin known as the Lakes offers boatmen navigable depths averaging five to six feet. This broad, protected lagoon is generally calm, and with the morning sun at his back an experienced flats skipper has little trouble following any of the seven deeper and darker channels that meander from the Lakes to the Atlantic.

But approached from the south, on the ocean side, the place has quite a different feeling. Even in windless weather, the heave of oceanic swells never ceases, and small-boat passengers are quite aware of these surging reminders that the Atlantic is indeed a vast and awesome place. But for me, the sheer drama of the Seven Sisters topography is so captivating that it tends to dominate all thought, even erasing my own self-imposed reminders about how and what I should cast if a fish presents itself.

To the west, on the ocean side near Man Key, there is a stretch of pale sand that transforms to emerald, azure, and turquoise as the sun rises, tides change, currents manifest, and winds shift. There are, I know, many reaches of such pale sands spilled the length of the Keys like pearl dust from a bucket. Because this one spills at the Atlantic's very rim, however, it is visited by creatures of the deep: great dark shapes that glide in superlative silence from the vast violet secret to the south onto the shallows of this luminous transparent reach. I have seen barracuda lying long and as still as stone pillars under a sun that marks each jewel set in every cuda's silver flank. Oceanic sharks cruise on thin-water missions charged with portents of violence, weaving search patterns of shadows as they glide from channel to flat, from flat to channel and back.

And tarpon come to play in each of the seven channels. Here they wait for the milling harvest a falling tide will sweep from the flats to the Atlantic. As May water warms to June's tropic temperatures, tarpon approach the Seven Sisters from all sides. Moving east from the Marquesas across the Boca Grande channel they slide along the ocean shoals, crossing that stretch of pale sand at the Sisters in small armadas of eight fish here, four here, another five there, moving like pods of sleek underwater livestock from one grazing place to another as they make their journey from mysterious source to mysterious destination, granting us this fleeting witness to their travels, this one quick look at a migration in progress.

Like sentries at a mountain pass, flats anglers will stake off along the entire reach of the Seven Sisters and wait for tarpon to come to them. It is a chancy business. Picking a place to drive a push pole deep into the marl so the flats skiff can be made fast to it with a line off her stern is a gamble as volatile as any in Vegas. While there is a kind of pattern to the history of tarpon past—"They liked this spot last year."—there is only the slimmest assurance that the fish may come this way again. Theirs is never a predetermined day. So many natural variables combine with a tarpon's mercurial persona that prediction becomes akin to witchcraft. What feels lucky is almost as effective as any computation of recent tarpon history.

There are, however, certain places at the Sisters favored by certain guides, just as there are certain shoals in the Marquesas and still more on each fishy flat in the back country. For although the number of Lower Keys flats guides increases each season, there is still room for professional courtesies, some as complex as a sacred tea ceremony. An angler, for example, should not fish a channel if a flats skiff has already staked off at its entrance. The unwritten rules are complex and require considerable understanding of how tarpon travel; an angler should not, as a general practice, move between a flats boat and the expected approach path of tarpon groups. But to do the right thing in such cases, an angler must have the experience to know the approach patterns for each particular flat. Alone in my skiff, for example, I would surely be cursed by several senior guides as I unwittingly cruised across proprietary space looking for fishing room.

The considerable courtesies and allegiance to protocols observed so agreeably by experienced flats guides always impresses me. As an alumni of trolling under the Montauk light, where as many as two hundred boats criss-crossed the same cramped confluence of Long Island tide rips in their hunt for bluefish and striped bass, I got my experience as a helmsman in a tense environment of near misses, cut lines, shouted curses, and, every now and then, the *whap!* of a heavy saltwater lure purposely cast at the boat as a deterrent to further bullish maneuvering. By contrast, the courtly behavior of skiff guides in the Lower Keys sets standards Montauk has never known and would never live with.

Jeffrey, by nature, is a considerate and gentle man who strenuously defends and observes local protocols even though he is as competitive about finding fish for his anglers as any guide in the nation. Like the very best of the relatively few professionals who take other folks fishing day after day after day, Jeffrey is genuinely pleased and gratified when he puts his people into fish. And when his anglers hook up and all goes well, the exuberance, the smile, the congratulations that Jeffrey articulates are real, just as the frowns and the discouraged expressions are real when he has a skimpy day, although he tries hard to keep the frowns from surfacing. This enduring empathy for each angler that comes aboard is the mark of an exceptional guide, and it is often the first of the fine points to be corroded over the years. Jeffrey's grace and enthusiasms, as every angler he has fished will tell you, are still shiny bright, fresh as a raindrop.

I know, because if there is an angler who has pushed Jeffrey's good nature to the wall, it is I. Take the sorry history of my tarpon quest; if ever there was a saga of slop, I have recorded it from the *Waterlight*'s casting platform in the bow. Even the riches of the Seven Sisters could not move against the tide of pre-destined failure that appears to be my tarpon fate.

Poling west on a fine late-May morning across the flats between Sister Four and Sister Five, Jeffrey calls out information and instruction as we ease toward the channel at Sister Five. As always, I wait on the bow, certain that this is to be the day when my tarpon curse will be lifted. Fly rod at the ready, knees shaking, wrist cocked, sweat building, I recite my endless internal litany of dos and don'ts, arranging each of them in confused order in my consciousness, mumbling as I go, waving my rod tip tentatively, testing to be certain I am not standing on my own fly line, a doltish maneuver I have managed more often than not.

"Tarpon rolling in the channel!" Jeffrey calls, his voice crisp. "About two o'clock."

"I'm going to ease up to the edge and turn the bow so you can cast to eleven."

Poling more steadily, Jeffrey sets the *Waterlight* on a gliding course toward the darker channel waters, flowing like a river toward the sea on an ebbing tide. I can see tarpon now. That familiar opalescence tints their silvery shoulders and backs as they roll. What serendipitous timing: as the great fish move toward the sea we move toward the channel at a spot that will intersect the school. Even for me, the cast will be easy.

"Cast now!" Jeffrey calls, with emphasis on the "now."

I do, an effort devoid of skill, but functional. My fly lands in the channel's center and quickly drifts with the tide.

Bang! A strike.

Rattling its gills, the tarpon leaps, just a few feet off our rail. I bow to it, wonder of wonders.

Falling into the channel, the fish begins a sudden, surging run toward the ocean. My rod bends sharply, then straightens, as light and as empty as air. How well I know the feeling.

"Shit, he's gone," I tell Jeffrey, who already knows.

Poling across to the flat, he stakes off and climbs down from his poling platform and comes to the bow where he begins to examine my fly line and broken leader.

As he reaches the leader's end, sliding each inch through his fingers, he says, "Wind knot."

The two words are a euphemism for the effect sloppy casting can have on a leader. It is never the wind that ties the knots, it is what the wind will do if the angler gives it the chance. Lack of line speed, the single most essential element of every decent cast, often means the leader will double back on itself in a gossamer monofilament tangle. Loops form as discipline dissolves and, every now and then, the fly itself drops through a loop and the result is a half-hitch in the leader, a knot no larger than a pinhead when it's drawn taut, a knot all but invisible yet easily discovered by an angler's fingertips run the leader's length in the kind of diligent inspection that becomes routine for every experienced fly fisherman. Well, every reasonably intelligent, alert, non-day-dreaming experienced fly fisherman, that is.

Jeffrey's fingertips are doing what mine should have done and he has found the crimped remains of a wind knot at its break. "A knot like that cuts your leader's integrity by half," he explains. The tarpon, whose leap is a vision of force firmly planted in my consciousness, appeared to be at least sixty pounds. The damaged leader began life as fifteen-pound test; the knot tied by my clumsy casting cut that to something less than eight pounds, not enough to hold a strong, large fish tormented by a hook in its jaw.

Jeffrey does not intend his sigh to ride so heavily on the midday air. But it does, a long note of disappointment and chagrin sounded in the empty aftermath of one more successful hunt by the guide and yet one more rather incredible fumble by the cursed angler from hell.

67

"What say we stake off and have some lunch," Jeffrey says, a note of genuine enthusiasm returning at the thought of the sandwiches Jean has packed for us both.

Crossing Sister Five we stake off near the edge of the flat that borders it on the west. We are on the Atlantic side, close enough to the sea to feel the echo of today's gentle swells. To the south and west, a far horizon spills; we are so near the ocean edge that we can look west past the southern rim of Man Key off toward the distant shoals that trapped the galleons of the Spanish Main and spread their cargoes across shifting sands only now being swept aside by torrents of pumped water, energy, lives, exotic equipment, and dollars consumed by man's eternal quest for buried treasure.

At peace, miles from the submerged bars of silver and gold scattered like chaff across a wheat field, we have our own treasure to contemplate as we drink our Gatorade and munch on cold sliced chicken and pumpernickel. Off to our west is that emerald expanse of pale sand, gleaming like a bright, blank page torn from the book of the sea.

"This is a good spot for lunch," Jeffrey explains. "If any fish move across this flat, we should be able to see them in time to make a cast."

I am too content with being relieved of the challenges faced from my casting platform on the bow. Lunch is, for me, more than a meal; it is an escape from the possibility of yet another failure, an escape I want to prolong, not shorten. But I have a strong intuition that my picnic cannot last. The recent past has taught me something about lunch on the flats. For no matter where I have paused or with whom I have been fishing, the lunch break inevitably tempts fish from their undersea keeps and emboldens them to meander by our skiff as if paying a social call during the one time of the fishing day when they are certain of a pleasant and harmless exchange of views: the fish looking up as we look down.

Not too long ago John Graves and I were parked a few miles southwest of this very spot, stopped for a respite and a repast after a long, long poling trek across the flats from the ruined breakwater east of Crawfish Key all the way to the flats south of Woman Key. We had hunted for tarpon since early morning, had seen a few but none that we considered in casting range. But just minutes after we eased our aching carcasses into the forward corners of John's compact skiff a pair of tarpon passed within ten feet of our inshore gunwale. A six-year-old could have reached them, and even an inexperienced angler would have had a better than fifty-fifty chance of dropping a fly far enough in front of the moving fish so one of the monsters need only open its awesome maw to engulf the hook that could make it captive.

But John and I could only look and remain quite stunned by our realization that a pair of creatures so wild, so huge, so lovely, so free, so elusive, and so radiantly silver under the noon-high sun had come almost within reach of our outstretched arms and then moved on as implacably as great underwater engines on a mission beyond our ken. We two could only watch their silent passing, look at each other, grimace, and then laugh.

That was but one of the flats lunches that produced fish from nowhere. There have been too many for me ever to expect I'll finish an uninterrupted sandwich. So when Jeffrey jumps to his feet, points, and yells, "Here comes a school of tarpon!" I am less galvanized than the situation warrants. I am, in fact, so content with my lunch-hour security that I tell Jeffrey, "You give them a try. I'll never get collected in time."

Which is partially true. I am in the stern, Jeffrey is in the bow and already has a rod close by. The larger part of the truth, however, is my reluctance to risk yet another tarpon failure. I can still hear the disappointment and chagrin in Jeffrey's voice when he said "wind knot."

"Go on, Cap," I say, putting some gristle in my tone, "get up there and give them a shot."

Picking up his fine, eleven-weight Winston rod fitted with its Abel reel, Jeffrey steps up on the bow. "There they are, there, about two o'clock, inside us, crossing the flats."

Looking north toward the Lakes I see the tarpon—probably six or eight fish that remind me of a small flight of wild geese in their loose formation. I get the same thumping in my chest, the same whole-body tremble, quickness of breath and lighter head that I once felt in those Bridgehampton potato-field pit blinds when I looked toward a violet eastern dawn and saw the velvet silhouettes of Canada geese moving toward us across the sky, their wonderfully wild calls insistent as the great birds tried to awaken our stupid, mute decoys standing on peg legs among new green shoots of winter wheat.

There was always the question waiting to be answered: Would the geese be deceived and turn, wings extended, web feet lowered to brake their creaky descent as they soared at the brink of death. Or, at the final moment would suspicion prevail and return the flock safely to the dawn.

We set out no decoys for tarpon, but Jeffrey knows the patterns of their movements. He has seen other schools like this one on other hundreds of days on this flat and scores more. "They'll turn when they hit the channel," he says. "They'll turn and follow the edge. They'll be coming our way."

In its cloudless sky, the high sun illuminates the thin water, gives it a rare transparency on this windless midday, makes it a kind of liquid air that sustains the tarpon flight, a squadron of long, dark space ships gliding toward us from another universe.

When it reaches the deep violet of the Five Sister channel, the formation wheels in a slow-motion turn. Now the missiles are aimed at the *Waterlight* as surely as if their course had been plotted for them by the same fates that have, so often, blessed Jeffrey and me with fish.

When tarpon travel undisturbed and at their ease they move at a serene meander, like Sunday strollers on a sunny avenue after church, their course firm for their family dinner at the grand table set with once-a-week silver. There is a sense of direction to their movements. But the movements are gentle, quite deliberate, as if the fish expect to meet acquaintances along the way and want to be able to stop and exchange pleasantries without appearing flustered by the interruption. But all serenity shatters the instant the travelers sense any imbalance in the harmonies of their accustomed environment. A shadow's dash as an angler raises an arm with the sun at his back, the reverberating vibrations of a too-heavy footstep or the crack of a guide's pole let fall against the edge of the poling platform—any anomaly sprung from the total anomaly of a skiff converts a tarpon meander to the chaos of shattered plate glass: silver fragments of the great fish cascade across the underwater sky as tarpon take flight, their Sunday stroll now a rocketing escape, an explosive surge of such breathtaking speed that all memory of the creatures at peace vanishes with them, lost in the faceless depths where, just an infinite moment ago, tarpon grazed like sheep in a field.

This skiff is stationary; we are staked off here for lunch. These tarpon are moving toward us, we are not gliding toward them. Circumstance is, once more, working in our favor.

From his bow casting-platform, Jeffrey has a superlative view of the tarpon group. The sun is over his shoulder, the breeze flutters just enough to animate the water's surface, not enough to frustrate visibility. Standing still as stone, Jeffrey raises no alarms and the fish continue to meander our way.

Just before they reach the outer boundary of their sensor's range, perhaps one hundred feet, Jeffrey raises his arm and begins his first false cast. Like every experienced flats fly fisherman, he has learned how to get an impressive amount of line in the air on the first sweep of his arm. With the vigorous motion of his back cast, a powerful arc of arm and body that is uniquely Jeffrey's, he gets another thirty feet of line on the move. Now he has about sixty feet aloft and I marvel.

On his final cast, the fly shoots almost ninety feet, dropping gently on the surface just far enough in front of the meandering tarpon to allow it to sink a foot or so. The lead fish is not interested, but the second in the loose formation veers slightly off course, opens its maw, and engulfs the Black Death pattern that Jeffrey retrieves so intensely, stripping slowly so the fly opens and closes, a small butterfly on feathered wings.

At the take, Jeffrey strikes hard, holding fast to the line with his left hand, yanking the rod with surprising force, keeping it low and parallel to the deck. At the same instant, the tarpon responds and there is tumult and turmoil on the water's surface one hundred feet off the bow.

Jeffrey strikes the fish once again, harder this time than before, harder than I ever imagined a fish needs to be struck.

"He's on!" Jeffrey yells as he allows line to rip through his left hand while the rods bucks in his right. In yet another instant, loose fly line has vanished through the guides and Jeffrey raises his rod tip, leans backward a bit so the rod bows and line starts hissing from the reel.

73

"He's on the reel!"

Two hundred feet off the tarpon leaps clear, a silver beam suspended, then tumbling, shaking and twisting to the sea at the center of a white foam flower.

Like his strikes, Jeffrey's tarpon-fighting tactics are strenuous and aggressive. Grunting, sweating, straining himself and his equipment, maintaining constant pressure and never relinquishing the initiative, he dominates the ninety-pound fish. Within twenty-five minutes, the tarpon is alongside, on its side, so stunned by the encounter that it allows Jeffrey to reach a hand inside its open mouth, a hand that grips the lower jaw and lifts most of the almost seven feet of the fish clear of the surface and holds it so I can snap a photograph of the angler and his trophy.

Sliding the fish gently back into the sea, still holding it tightly by its lower jaw, his deeply tanned right hand all but engulfed by the tarpon's maw, Jeffrey works the fly loose with his left hand and lets the fish submerge. Sliding his hand back toward the tail, and taking a fresh grip at the tail's base, he moves the big fish back and forth slowly, pushing water through its gills, helping to provide the oxygen that will speed the tarpon's recovery from what, for the fish, has been a fifteen-round fight that ended in a knockout.

In moments the broad tail and torpedo torso convulse with the tarpon's efforts to escape. Jeffrey releases his grip and gives the fish a shove. Fanning its tail a bit sluggishly, the tarpon moves across the flats, its nose pointed toward the darker waters of the open Atlantic.

"He's okay," Jeffrey says. "He's going to be fine." He is especially relieved because no sharks have shown up. More than once, the predators' sensitive receptors have gotten a message of distress from hooked tarpon fought from the *Waterlight*. One large hammerhead cut a trophy tarpon in half just as the angler was about to break the fish off. Instead, the picture Jeffrey took shows the fisherman holding the bloody head half of what had been a 160-pound fish just moments before the shark moved in, took hold and shook its great jaws violently enough to tear the tarpon asunder.

As the tarpon vanishes, I sit down to nibble on the grapes and cookies Jean packed for our dessert. I tell Jeffrey, "Congratulations. You make it look easy. But I learned something from watching. I would never strike a fish that hard. Even now that I've seen it done, I'm not sure I can do it. I'd be afraid I might pull the hook loose."

"No," Jeffrey says, "no, you won't. The inside of a tarpon's mouth is concrete block. Your fly is not going to stay there unless you make sure you set the hook. And just once is not enough. Two times, three times, that's the only way to be sure. And the line must be tight when you strike. Remember that. Your left hand must pull the line tight. Otherwise, your strike is meaningless."

Nodding my comprehension, but not my assurance that I can

heed such sensible instructions, I go back to my grapes. With the warm sun on my shoulders and the easy rolling of the *Waterlight* on the ocean's all but imperceptible swells adding a kind of silent lullaby to my post-lunch torpor, I'm thinking how splendid to be so utterly at ease, so close to nap time.

"Come on, Cap, get up here," Jeffrey calls, holding out the rod. "It's your turn. There'll be more tarpon on the way soon."

This time I cannot rationalize my way out of the challenge. Jeffrey, no matter how much I press, will not fish again. He took his shot only because he knew I was discouraged by the wind-knot fiasco and needed some recovery time. I make my way to the bow and there I stand, wondering for perhaps the fifteenth time if I'll ever get this right.

"Permit! Permit!" Jeffrey's yell bangs against my ears.

"Out there," he calls, pointing. "There at eleven o'clock. See them. Can you see them?"

For an old fart, my eyes are still in good condition, especially at long range. Most of the time I have no trouble seeing fish, or anything else that's more than a foot from my nose. But I'm having trouble now picking up these permit Jeffrey claims are there.

For one thing, just the word "permit" is inclined to throw me off. It carries such a burden. These are, as the folklore of the flats has emphasized over the years, the most wary, the most difficult, the most inexplicable, the most contrary and cursed fish a fly-caster can meet in thin water. I have heard countless tales from permit fanatics like Nat Reed and others about the permit's obdurate refusals of flies flawlessly presented. "He looked, but he wouldn't eat," is the popular shorthand history of a day spent casting to the muscular, flat-sided pewter-hued fish with bulldog jaws and the strength of a fast freight train. Absorbing permit dock-talk and bar-chat during time spent at both, I have come to understand that only a relative handful of first-class anglers have landed a permit on a fly. Thousands of fishermen better than I have never even had one strike.

And now Jeffrey is urging me to cast a tarpon fly to what he tells me is a trio of "big" permit that I have yet to locate.

"Cast now! Cast now!" he orders. "Cast to eleven."

Squinting toward eleven, I see what I think are the fish: dark shapes against a mottled bottom. It is their motion I see more than their profiles. They are, I notice, swimming our way.

Helped by a breeze that has gathered a bit of pep, my cast falls a bit short. It is, nevertheless, good enough to put the fly directly in front of the trio's implacable progress.

"He sees it!" Jeffrey yells. His excitement is beginning to communicate and my legs start their standard tremble.

"Twitch the fly. Twitch it just a bit."

I follow instructions.

"He's going to eat it. He's eating it! Strike him. Strike him!"

I produce a somewhat clumsy rendition of the same striking technique I watched Jeffrey lay on that tarpon an hour or so ago. In my opinion, I don't need even that. This permit, this one witless permit among his tens of thousands of wise and wary brethren, this single simpleton hooks himself.

And, like the retarded giant that he is, he scarcely realizes what he's done. Swallowing the fly, the fish turns casually, thinking perhaps he may find more tidbits.

My strike, as woebegone as it is, sounds a distant alarm. The permit shakes his sturdy, blunt boxer's head just a bit, deciding now to get rid of whatever it is he thought he'd swallow.

But the hook, at last, is set. And, at last, the permit feels steel. And he's off, rocketing furiously across the flats.

"Careful, careful." How much anxiety there is in Jeffrey's voice. "Watch the line. Watch the line. Keep your left hand out. Hold it out away from the rod."

The overload of slack fly line I had piled on the deck (I'm always certain *this* will be the cast that sends it all through the guides) is zipping through my left hand at a dangerous rate. In the instant of true recognition that I am now fast to a hefty and definitely alarmed permit, I am also aware of how easily a loop of slack line can snarl and catch—on the rod butt, around my ankle, anywhere. It's happened before with tarpon. How much more likely disaster seems with a permit.

But the same whimsical fates who sent a slow-learner permit to meet me on this late-May afternoon decide it's going to be my day, at least from here on, no matter what.

"He's on the reel!" Jeffrey is more joyous than I've ever heard him. Joyous and a bit incredulous, as well he should be.

This bully of a permit hauls ass across the flats and begins a series of thumping maneuvers designed to snap the twelve-pound-test leader, rip loose the hook, or somehow so confuse me that I yank too hard in one direction or not enough in another. What the permit cannot know is that Jeffrey's instructions are given every thirty seconds or so, and always in anticipation of what the permit is about to do, not in reaction to what it has already done. Thanks to my guide, I can stay a half-step ahead of this fish, which is just where I should be if I am going to prevail.

This is a stubborn and determined fish, apparently unaware that I hold the aces. This permit may not be intelligent but it is definitely unfazed. And, after a half hour of retrieving line and then watching it vanish as the fish makes yet another run, I am losing my confidence. Soon, I tell myself, something's going to have to give here, and it's going to be at my end of the line.

Instead, it is the permit who first loses his pep.

As I crank, hoist, and retrieve line foot-by-foot, the fish gets closer and closer to the boat. He has entered the hazard circle, the short-range arena where stress is intensified because it all must be absorbed by just a few feet of line and leader. It is in this quivering time zone that most fish are lost.

Jeffrey's words are a shower now, a constant flood of reassurance and instruction.

He stands at the rail, a long-handled, wide-mouthed, deep-bellied net in his hands. When he knows it can be done, he sweeps the net surely in one long stroke, raises it from the water, straining now because there in the net's enfolding meshes is a permit, my permit in all its silver-violet splendor, gleaming in the streaming sun.

Jeffrey rests the net handle on the gunwale so the permit can stay underwater.

"A permit on a fly!" he shouts. "You got a permit on a fly!"

I'm smiling. I'm happy. I'm delighted. And I'm so totally grateful that I did not make a mistake grievous enough to cost me and Jeffrey this shimmering moment.

Carefully removing the fly, hooked solidly in the tough skin of the permit's heavy jaw, Jeffrey weighs the fish. "Twenty-five pounds," he calls. "That's a fine permit."

Then he jumps overboard with his camera, wades backward on the flat until I and the permit fill his viewfinder. "Click." There we are together for now and always, against the blue sky, cotton-puff clouds and bright water of that incredible day, me and the permit, he definitely the handsome one with his colors true, the tint of chrome yellow along his belly edge, great black orb of an eye, sleek, solid body and fine, wide tail.

I botched my tarpon chance, but not this one. Once more, the unexpected has blessed us.

It is such a heady moment, I all but lose control. Moments after Jeffrey has released the fish and made certain it's in good shape, I say, "Hey, that's a tarpon and a permit. Let's go look for a bonefish and we'll have a grand slam."

Jeffrey is a bit giddy himself. "Why not," he says, and cranks up the *Waterlight* for a spin along the ocean edge to a flat just off Ballast Key, where, once every great while, bonefish visit.

They are not there this day, but then neither of us really thought they would be. Nor do we care.

On the way home, whipping through the Lakes, isolated by the Evinrude's snarl and the roar of the wind pushed past by our 50-mph ride, I tell myself I still have a tarpon to catch. That fish is still out there, and will always be until I either get lucky, stop making mistakes, or both. Except for today, my recent history doesn't leave much room for hope.

But today: Hey, a permit on a fly.

Dumb luck or no, I can live with that. For a long while, too.

SIX

Michael Pollack first appeared in the sky above me. Last in a short line of two or three anglers in their skiffs waiting for the hoister that would lift our boats to their dry storage berths at the Garrison Bight Marina, I was bantering back and forth with Jeffrey, whose *Waterlight* has its own, permanent place at the marina dock.

"Cap, this is Mike Pollack," Jeffrey said, waving toward a substantial presence on the dock. Looking up, I saw a round, friendly face atop a robust, friendly frame. From the first, Mike reminded me of a young Teddy Roosevelt; he had that same arrangement of features and he instantly communicated the same hearty enthusiasms I have always assigned to Teddy. If Mike had said, "Bully!" I wouldn't have been the least surprised.

I learned he had recently arrived from Ennis, Montana, where he spends his springs and summers running a small fishing camp and tackle shop on the Madison River, quite an enterprise for a man who has a few years to go before he discovers forty. Like several other Keys guides who have helped build the Montana/Keys connection, Mike made his first trip to Florida three winters ago and, I learn, has come to Key West to complete the apprenticeship and paperwork that will allow him to become a registered flats guide.

As I exchange questions and answers with him, his head and face and frame outlined against the afternoon sky, the sketchy beginnings of an understanding emerge that will, as days pass, bring yet another splendid bonus: days on the water handed to me on the lovely platter of fortunate circumstance—circumstance I'm certain Jeffrey helped to arrange.

"I need an angler to practice on," Mike told me. "I need to put someone in the bow of my skiff, someone who will be just as intense as the anglers I'll get when I get my guide's papers and my new skiff. You want to let me practice on you?"

I decide I really *am* the Blanche DuBois of fishermen. Here is yet another stranger extending me a kindness, more than a kindness, a miracle. I get to fish the flats and, at the same time, perform something of a service for the man who guides me, whose boat I'm fishing from and whose husky self is up there on the poling platform, eyes peeled, trying to find fish for me. How's that for a stroke of luck.

84

In return, the least I can do is to perform well as an angler. But I soon see I have not quite made the transition from my clumsy self to skilled fly-caster. Take that first mid-morning with Mike on the flats along the east side of Archer Key Basin; it was one of the few late-December days of settled weather that followed a prolonged cold spell (well, cold for Key West), and barracuda were crowded on the flats like gamblers at a Vegas convention, darting here and there, full of joy and excitement at the return of the sun they seek so earnestly during winter's shorter days.

But despite the vast gathering—more barracuda than I've seen before or since in one spot—I never hooked up. And I was casting deadly, long, luminous, green synthetic-fiber flies hand-tied by Jeffrey, a surefire lure he calls the Cuda Libre because there are a few strands of sparkle woven among the day-glo green.

Somehow, even so finely equipped, I just couldn't get it together. Several times I waited too long to begin casting; when I did, the cuda were too close. They watched me false cast and then took off, just as *the* cast was still in mid-flight. And once, at the far north end of the basin, where, at dead low tide, water tumbles from the flats in what amounts to a rushing stream, I cast to a barracuda who turned, his bold colors flashing with the adrenalin of the chase, and began slashing through the shallows as he fought to reach my fly. He had a ways to go, and thinking my next cast might make his job easier, I hauled back to pick up and throw. But I miscalculated the cuda's speed. He struck just as I hauled back. I literally yanked the skinny fly from his snapping jaws just in time to miss the strike.

Mike was, understandably, nonplussed. But, like so many of the quiet, good-natured, open-hearted folks from Montana, he said not a word. I apologized, trying to keep my new fishing friend, and told him I was doing my best to get him in shape for the job ahead.

"When you begin your professional career," I said, "you'll find everything easier than today. There aren't more than a handful of anglers in the world who can jerk a fly free of the closing jaws of a fish in a feeding frenzy."

It was one of those incidents with staying power. I've been Mike's angler several times since, and each time I relive that trip. I call it "my incredible inept." I don't talk about it, but I think about it, just as I think about it on this bright and promising late-April morning as Mike pilots his idling skiff along the canal on the way to yet another effort to find me a fish.

Today, however, we are going to concentrate on tarpon.

I can't help but think that Mike is either very brave, a glutton for punishment, or extremely patient, kind, and forgiving. He has heard my tarpon history told and retold by both Jeffrey and myself. And I'm certain that although he never mentions it, my gross mismanagement of that barracuda moment is as vividly imprinted in his memory as it is in mine.

And yet he shares this day as enthusiastically, as generously, as if I had no dismal past, no curse of the deep forever on my

86

shoulders. Instead, he's cheerful. "Now this is a fine day," he says, examining a blue sky approvingly as we glide past mangroves and egrets on our way to begin our quest in Bluefish Channel.

There may have been a few bluefish taken over the years in the waters around the Lower Keys, but not more than a few. The waters are too warm too much of the time. But if a large blue was caught, it must have been in Bluefish Channel; names in this part of the world are not assigned by some anonymous Geodetic Survey mapmaker. They spring from native usage, regional legend, or, every now and then, a fisherman's whimsy. Barracouta Key is the archaic spelling of the mischievous species that hangs out in the vicinity, just as the Mud Keys are named for the consistency of the bottom around them. As for Woman Key, well, you'll have to find the fisherman who named her.

Bluefish Channel is the easternmost of three neighboring, parallel channels just to the east of Key West Harbor. Jack Channel, where a world-record tarpon was taken years ago, and Calda Channel are west of Bluefish, and each of them is, at one time or another during the tarpon's spring migration, a well-traveled tarpon waterway. Flanked by flats on both sides, Bluefish is a relatively short, narrow reach of deeper water that dead-ends on the flats just off Fleming Key and empties into the Gulf to the north. It's my guess (and that's just what it is) that tarpon move in from the Gulf on the incoming tide and stay there, knowing that as the tide falls, shrimp, mullet, pinfish, crabs, and other tarpon favorites will have to leave the diminishing flats for the deeper water where the big fish wait. Otherwise, I ask myself, why would tarpon go to all the trouble of working their way along such a narrow and irregular passage?

As Mike eases his skiff across the flats east of the channel, quietly, making sure not to disturb any tarpon that may or may not be lounging in Bluefish depths, he and I both see the same fish roll, there in the middle of the channel.

A rolling tarpon is a fine sight that gets even better when you have a tarpon fly ready to cast.

"There's a roller," Mike says, just as I open my mouth to say "Hey, there's one." Both of us, I'm sure, are thinking, "This could be the day," and the morning has just begun. Like me, Mike has yet to land a tarpon in three years of trying. Thus the thought that our drought may be broken right here in Bluefish Channel just a ten-minute boat ride from Key West gooses our adrenalin and trembles our extremities.

As quietly as he can, given the tensions of the moment, Mike stakes off and lets our tether grow longer and longer until the breeze at our backs drifts us to the channel edge where a good saltwater fly-caster can cast almost all the way across the darker, deeper water.

Mike can do it. My casts cover about three-fourths of the distance, but because the tarpon we keep seeing are rolling in the center of the waterway, I'm confident the fish are within range. So is Mike, and both of us cast with vigor, he from atop the poling platform in the stern while I work from my accustomed location on the bow.

Honed by several weeks of dreaming about just such a morning—here we are, along with a bunch of big fish—my intensity all but gets the best of me, I'm trying to cast precisely as Lefty Kreh tells me I should when he talks to me from my television set, and I'm trying to retrieve with the same butterfly rhythms that Jeffrey teaches. Meanwhile, the tarpon roll every now and then, close enough to convince me that at least a few of them have seen our offerings, especially mine. But they don't appear interested. I don't feel so much as a bump. Nor does Mike.

"Fuckers won't eat," I observe after a half-hour of what I'm certain is flawless technique.

"Seems that way," Mike replies. "I'm going to change flies."

This is one of fly fishing's most agreeable attributes. No matter what the circumstances, if fish won't strike, the angler can always blame the fly. Even an underprivileged angler generally carries more than two-dozen different patterns, enough to fish each one a half-hour for two days around the clock, convinced that when the right fly is, at long last, chosen, the fish will be hooked.

"I think I will, too." It takes me about fifteen minutes. Seven minutes into the process, one of the largest tarpon we've seen rolls just off the bow. It's a sustained and dignified presence that allows my perception of details: the jutting thrust of its lower jaw; the confirmation of its silver-dollar scales; and the sibilance of the air so delicately expelled as the great head

89

emerges like Neptune's from the sea, a single immense and impressively fathomless jet-black eye staring from it directly at my ineffectual self hunched over a leader that is, at the moment, stripped and utterly harmless.

"Isn't that always the way," comments Mike, like me still in the process of the fly-changing ritual.

I tell myself the great fish is still there as I finally complete the transition from the fly called a Cockroach to a red-and-yellow number named the Seaducer, which I stand and cast with renewed commitment and pumping energy.

Without success.

Not a touch.

Meanwhile, in a ballet telepathically tuned to the rise and fall of our expectations, tarpon roll somewhere within our vision precisely when we are convinced there are none within a mile. We are being teased with such skill that I am convinced the tarpon have conspired to tantalize. Always just out of range and forever wary of every fly, no matter how superbly presented or how deceitfully tied, the fish of Bluefish Channel hold us here, harmless. We could, I decide, stay the day and come up empty.

Mike arrives at the same conclusion about the same time. He and I apparently operate on similar thresholds. "The hell with this," he says, stepping down from the poling platform, stowing his rod, and beginning the process that will get us underway. "Let's go slide across Calda Bank and see if we can find some big barracuda on the flats. I swore I'd stick with tarpon. I promised up and down I'd never fool around with cuda again. But, hey, we might as well give it a shot. At least we'll get some action."

Mike is talking himself into the plan, not me. I'm easy. I'll cast to cuda any day. Given my tarpon history, it's a wonder I'm still playing their games.

The flats of Calda Bank run west from the Gulf entrance to Bluefish Channel and end at the deep water of Northwest Channel, the primary shipping lane running from Key West Harbor to the Gulf proper. Because it is impressively deep and connects directly with the Atlantic, Northwest Channel is also a favorite travel lane for the largest oceanic fishes: tarpon, permit, barracuda, and sharks. And because Calda Bank has this channel along one edge and the Gulf on another, it is frequently visited by outsize underwater travelers looking for a few moments in the shallows where they can feel the sun on their great, broad backs.

Surveying the golden sweep of these flats on a day that has continued to maintain perfection, I stand on the bow, cuda rod and cuda fly at the ready, as Michael poles.

"There's a school of big fish at twelve o'clock," he calls, his tone ascending in volume and excitement.

Yes, indeed there is. I can see them now. Like Mike, I assume they are barracuda, in this case, some of the largest I have ever seen. But they are a long way off when we spot them and as they continue on their course and we ours, I realize our remarkable mistake.

"Tarpon! Those are tarpon!"

Now the fish, and they are unmistakably tarpon, huge ones, seven of them, each more than a hundred pounds, have reached the intersect where I must begin my cast or miss the chance altogether.

"This is a *cuda* fly!" I yell back at Mike, telling him what he already—and so despairingly—knows.

"Cast anyway!" he yells. "Cast now!"

Somewhat better than it was a year ago, but not as good as I hoped it would be, my casting form and the gentle breeze combine to drop the big, green fly about six feet from the lead fish in the school. These are happy fish fresh from the deep and there is a casual grace to the movements of the first tarpon as he curves languidly off course, gliding toward my fly. There is an infinitely fleeting moment when I have a right to think this Cuda Libre will perform a miracle.

But the moment sags in less than a heartbeat. Flies, in this case anyway, do make a difference. One glance and the tarpon rejoins the school and the wonderfully wild and dignified procession continues, moving past us and on toward Calda Channel.

Mike is livid. "Never, never, never again," he shouts. "No more barracuda flies on this boat. None. Not ever. If you want to catch tarpon, you have to fish for tarpon. It's just that simple. This is about the fifth time I've missed a shot because I decided to screw around with goddamn barracuda . . ."

His rampage dwindles to a mutter as I stow the cuda rod.

We cruise the flat for another hour, hoping for a reprieve, another school of trophy tarpon sent to bless our day. But the search is grim; each of us knows we have missed a moment only the fortunate are likely to see once a season. Twice in one afternoon is more than we should expect and we know it.

"How about the channel at Archer Key Basin?" Mike says as the afternoon swells to maturity and begins its roll toward evening. In fifteen minutes we cross Northwest Channel and ease into the narrow opening of a nameless cut between Northwest's markers and Archer Key.

Incredibly, the day grows more contented as it wanes. The well-mannered breeze that was seldom disorderly through the morning has now all but vanished and taken the clouds with it. We are adrift, riding the last of an ebb tide on a silken surface. Looking down as the small channel unrolls beneath us, we can see turtle grass wave and coral heads stand at attention.

And barracuda, scores of them driven to this deep by a falling tide that leaves them no choice. Mike mutters, but I'm not listening. Halfway along the channel, I see a tarpon roll, and then another. I cannot believe this day's fates can be so tolerant.

From his poling platform, Mike sees them too. I know what's coming.

"Okay, John," he says, "get up there and take your shot."

As we get closer, a lower sun angling in from our right, each individual fish is a silver-blue form set in the lighter blue of the ten-foot depths. There are perhaps fifteen tarpon, small ones.

"They're babies," Mike says. "Aren't they beautiful. And they're in range."

I cast the Seaducer and it has scarcely touched the satin water when it becomes the center of a splash. As the tarpon strikes I stand paralyzed with delight. By the time I react, the fly has been spit back at me.

Mike sighs. "They're not going anywhere," he says. "Strip back and cast again."

I do. And this time I'm ready for the strike. What a blessed day. A second fish pulls from the school, rushes the fly and *"Bang!"* it's on. I am, at long last, hooked up.

It is, indeed, a small fish. Its first jump reminds me of a hefty Atlantic salmon. And I am over-equipped. The lovely, stiff, twelve-weight, nine-foot rod John Graves built just for me on a Loomis blank is designed to cope with much larger fish, maybe even 150-pounders, and although I'm not certain I have the strength for that much tarpon, the rod does. It gives this juvenile little quarter, in spite of a game effort and several acrobatic jumps.

In ten minutes, the tarpon is alongside. Mike lifts it gently from the water with both hands and presents it to me; he is King Arthur handing a knight his first sword.

"You did it," he says. "You did it. Your first tarpon on a fly. Now hold it in your arms so I can take a picture. Hold it right across your chest."

I embrace the tarpon. It's about a twenty-pounder. Mike

94

clicks his camera twice, then I remove the fly and slip "my" tarpon back into the soft waters of the evening and watch as it moves slowly, gingerly toward deeper water. As it goes, the beat of its tail increases. The fish will be okay.

And I am more than okay. I am delighted. After three years, a barrier has been broken, a burden lifted, a benchmark inscribed as indelibly as those that record my first salmon, a son's graduation, or a daughter's wedding. This long, placid, and orchestrated day was a perfect prologue to this happy ending.

But there is still some daylight left, still some time to try to end Mike's three-year drought. We drift along the channel as he stands in the bow casting and I look down from the poling platform, trying my best to operate the single electric motor so the skiff will go where Mike tells me to take it.

By now, the tide has turned and the new flood carries us back the way we first came, toward Northwest Channel. We are almost at the joining, the place where this fishing day will surely end, when a tarpon rises unseen from the channel, bursts vertically from the surface, a silver missile launched on its own adrenalin, mouth agape with Michael's fly at the corner of its jaws. Gill plates rattle like chain mail in wet, windless air and Michael is quite suddenly totally involved with a meeting he never expected.

Instantly, he makes it a contest. Strong, stocky, and determined, Mike literally fights his fish. There is no moment when he relents. But this is a large fish, ninety to a hundred pounds, at least, and it does not surrender. Each time Mike turns its run, has the tarpon coming, the fish allows itself to be forced just so near the boat, then steams off, taking back the line Michael retrieved.

Michael sweats, puffs, heaves, leans, pulls, strains, and sweats some more. The sun is about to set when at last the fish is boated. This one is not easily lifted, but Mike will not be denied. He hoists it, finally, into his arms and this time I take the photographs.

After its release, the tarpon shoves across the flats to Northwest Channel. And when the tide carries the skiff into the same deeper water, Mike gives a great, explosive, exuberant shout and jumps overboard, clothes and all.

When we get back to my home, Mike grabs a six-pack and I take a bottle of wine and we walk around the corner to Jeffrey's to celebrate and live the day again. He shares the joy, but with an edge of regret he is too honest to try to disguise.

"I was hoping," he says from his chair on the deck under the twilight sky, "that you could be on my boat when you got your first tarpon."

I tell him, "Hey. This is just a starter tarpon. Hardly twenty pounds. I'm still waiting for a *tarpon* tarpon, and I'll be with you when I get it.

"That's when, not if."

SEVEN

As May moved toward Memorial Day, the first tropical depression of 1990 was born in the southeastern Atlantic, drifted west until it reached Cuba, and then turned north toward Key West. It was the same combination of weather systems that can, when conditions are more promising, grow to become a hurricane. Meteorologists tracked the depression with interest: their computers had already told them that hurricanes are more likely to favor South Florida and the Caribbean whenever rainfall off the coast of West Africa conforms to certain pre-established patterns.

This is the year, we were told, that those African rains will shape a new future for Atlantic hurricanes. Key West, and all South Florida, are now likely targets, as opposed to possible.

Listening to the reports and listening to the thirty-knot winds in the palm trees around our house, I began to believe that my starter tarpon was the first and last I would see. Booked at least a year ahead for every available fishing day in April, May, and June, Jeffrey's schedule is inflexible, and more than a year ago we had chosen May 27 and 28 as my two days. On the 25th I stood on our front porch marveling at the downpour cascading from our roof and watching a bedraggled flock of ibis huddle in a corner of the park across our street, trying to find shelter from the blustery gale.

The 26th was not much better, although the wind dropped toward the end of the day and the rain stopped around noon. There had been no fishing for anyone for three days.

At 5:30 on the morning of the 27th I arrive at Garrison Bight as planned, but full of questions and doubts about what the day will bring. Overhead, stars announce clear skies and a blush in the east indicates the sun will be bright. But storms like the one that has left Key West streets littered with palm fronds and frangipani blossoms do not exit cleanly. The tumult of their passing disturbs the seas and its creatures; normal behavior patterns are upset; fish that appeared regularly at this location on that tide often are nowhere to be found and it takes more than a single day of good weather to bring them back.

I'm certain Jeffrey is aware of this, but he will not articulate the slightest doubt. "It's going to be a great day!" he says as the *Waterlight* idles out of the harbor in the dark. "One of the best days of our lives."

This is pure Jeffrey. He begins every day determined to make it the best. It's as if his will can bend life into shape, can, by the sheer intensity of his enthusiasms, remove every moment from the path of all possible misfortune. It is contagious, this concentration on the positive, this love for where he is and what he does, this unflagging enjoyment. It takes more than a tropical depression to stifle Jeffrey's vitality, much more, and I am quickly won over. I stop worrying about where the tarpon may have been blown and start believing that we will find fish before most of Key West has had breakfast.

We are speeding west now, toward the darkest sky, toward the Marquesas twenty-five miles out there in the night. Jeffrey wants to be there first. He synchronizes his fishing with tarpon behavior: they are shy, more nocturnal than diurnal, and easily spooked by the sound of motors. Our best chance, as Jeffrey sees it, is to be the first and only boat, to approach quietly and to be in the one place where tarpon are most likely to surface. For years now he has bet on the Marquesas, the circle of hammocks and islands on the west side of the Boca Grande Channel, the last landfall west of Key West before the Tortugas. And for years he has remained convinced that the early angler gets the fish, which is why I padded into my kitchen at 4:30 this morning for a cup of coffee and some toast. It wouldn't do, I told myself, to keep Jeffrey waiting, not even a minute.

Because we leave an hour before sun-up, the sky is still murky when we reach Boca Grande Channel, one of the roughest holes in South Florida waters. Even on windless days, the clash of tides and currents pushing through the deep, narrow passage from the ocean to the Gulf creates short, random, lumpy seas that can rattle a small boat's seams. This morning's channel is a total disaster: swelling remnants of the storm mix with a chop from the southwest which, in turn, fights a swiftly flooding tide.

Jeffrey scarcely slows. We bounce hard from one short sea to the next. There is one tense, snarling moment when the *Waterlight*'s entire hull is airborne and the Evinrude's propellor blades whine miserably before we slam into the next choppy swell.

"That's called an air bite," Jeffrey explains when we reach the eastern tip of the Marquesas and slide into friendlier, more protected waters to collect ourselves and begin our tarpon quest. "We're the first boat here," he adds by way of further explanation.

In the unwritten rules of conduct for Key West flats guides, being first allows us to pick our spot, any spot in the entire rich array of the Marquesas' watery crossroads tarpon have favored over the centuries.

This morning we wait off the east shore along the rim of the flat that stretches toward the channel we have just crossed. This juncture of deep water and shoal is a tarpon highway. Migrating from the west and south, from the Atlantic to the Gulf, large schools cruise the edge of these flats like automobiles taking a wide curve in the road.

But this morning there is no traffic. As we watch and wait, other skiffs arrive and take their places. Soon, the entire Marquesas' perimeter will be ringed.

At eight-thirty, when our day is three hours old, Jeffrey says, "Well, I guessed wrong this morning." His voice and tone are their own Greek tragedy.

"I think the storm messed things up," I tell him, knowing how intensely he wants to find me a fish. For a moment I consider lowering the flames of our purpose. This has all come to too much, I tell myself. What does it matter if we don't succeed, if we head back tarponless. A great many anglers have done the same. I'm about to start a more light-hearted conversation aimed at keeping our endeavor in scale, but I stay silent. Jeffrey, I realize once again, is so committed he'll think any such rationalization on my part is a signal I'm ready to quit, and that he will not take.

We move on, first to the south side, then to the west, each the stage for some prior melodrama we shared. We were staked off on the south when that record tarpon ate my fly, took its run, and then came back so fast I looped line on my reel. And we were on the west when another great fish hooked up close to the boat and I botched clearing my loose fly line. Clumsy disasters both, and both unspoken as we return to the scenes of my crimes.

It is eleven, and we have seen one school of juveniles cavorting in the mouth of one of the several south-side channels. I

101

cast to the school and got a strike which I missed, a depressing omen.

"John, you've got to strike your fish much harder, much faster. You were standing there looking when that small fish hit. Remember now, keep your rod tip low, pointed directly at your line. Hold the line tight in your left hand, and move your rod low, parallel to the deck as hard as you can." Jeffrey takes my rod from me and demonstrates. "Give it all your energy. Put your back and shoulders in it."

He is a fine teacher, and sets high standards.

"Let's take a break," he says after a few minutes, and we stake off for lunch. It's a quiet meal. With the morning gone, it is all but impossible for Jeffrey's hopes to sustain. In his history, afternoons are not tarpon time.

Sandwiches gone, deck tidied, and motor running, the captain looks over the day's dwindling opportunities and asks, "Where do you want to try next?" as if I knew. It's a half-rhetorical query and I leave my half untouched. Jeffrey must decide.

"Let's go back to the east side again. Check it out. See if anything has changed with the tide. Okay?"

Of course okay.

This is the Atlantic, here to the east of the Marquesas. It is an oceanic edge we navigate here at this coral and marl outpost, this final wild jewel at the end of the Keys necklace. And we drive a distance offshore, leaving a wide band of open water between us and the shore so our passage will not disturb any of the anglers staked off on the flats or at the channel mouths.

As we turn east, at speed now, up on a plane, I look for the smudge of Boca Grande Key against the horizon, across the lumpy channel we'll have to transit one more time on our way home. I'm hoping, quietly, that it has settled a bit since our snarling, slamming dawn. And I'm peering, a trifle on the sly, to see if I can check the dimensions of the swells.

As I do, I pick up a bit of watery turmoil between us and the channel. The surface I can see looks ruffled, blown by its own internal wind. I have seen this before. It can mean fish are plowing these blue-green acres.

Then a tarpon leaps silver, then another.

Now I am certain. "Out there!" I call, "Out there!" pointing.

"Yes, I see."

"They are tarpon, aren't they?"

Jeffrey answers yes, but adds, "I don't know what has them so wild."

I haven't thought of the fish as ill-behaved. To me, their jumps and thrashing seem a larger-scale version of times off Montauk when a school of bluefish slashes its way through a couple of acres of bait. "We'll have to wait and see if they settle down," Jeffrey says.

He heads even further offshore at full throttle. A good half-mile beyond the continuing tarpon tumult, he swings east

103

again, leaves the fish a mile or so behind, and cuts back north toward the shore, slowing as we reach the edge of the flats, then shutting down. We drift in the swells as he navigates with his electric motors, keeping our bow facing the fish, closer now and moving steadily toward us.

"They should come this way," he tells me. He is a guide now, a man who has learned the invisible roads tarpon travel.

And he is right. As we drift, using the electric motors sparingly and only to hold our bow toward the approaching school, it becomes clear the tarpon mass will soon engulf us. It is a large school, perhaps two or three acres of fish, most of them thrashing, cutting water, leaping, and generally creating an awesome commotion. Awesome enough, certainly, to set my heart thumping, my hands atremble, and my knees likewise.

"I don't know what has these fish so frantic," Jeffrey calls from the poling platform, "but get ready to cast to eleven. Get ready. Start casting now!"

We are surrounded by huge tarpon. Their silver shapes hurtle across every corner of my vision. Like a sea within a sea, the waves of their tumultuous presence break over my consciousness. I am bewildered, without orientation, all but paralyzed.

"Cast to eleven. *Eleven!*" Jeffrey yells.

And I do. I see the pod of tarpon he sees. They are on the move and I am casting into the wind. But, as Jeffrey told me I must, I have been practicing and it shows. The fly drops in front of a moving fish. Without hesitation, a tarpon eats the Gurkha that Jeffrey tied the previous evening: "A foot soldier in our war on tarpon," he told me as he selected it.

I am part of that war. Remembering instructions, I strike and strike again, hard. "That's the way. That's the way." Jeffrey begins the instructions and encouragements that flow like a river from the stern.

The line begins to surge and rise.

"He's going to jump! Bow to him! Bow!"

I dip my rod tip to the water.

Far off, far, far off a silver pillar bolts upright from the sea, hovers an instant and tumbles into foam. Could that be my fish? It is, it must be. Already so much line gone.

This is a feisty, tough, and battling fish. It jumps—more than seven times, we count. It runs. And toward the end of its struggle moves into the shoal waters of the flats where Jeffrey is all but certain it will tug the line against a coral head and snap the frayed leader.

Jeffrey is behind me now as the fish comes closer. This is one guide who sees an end to frustration and does not want the final moments to change the course of events. Each move I make, each crank of the reel, each shift of counterbalance and direction is orchestrated by Jeffrey's encouraging instructions.

And, at the moment when the ache in my shoulders and the sweat in my eyes is persuading me that yes, this fish can still prevail, the tarpon is alongside, its great length almost at rest, a wild creature wearily at peace.

Gently, Jeffrey leans over the rail, removes the fly, hoists the tarpon high enough for me to hold it a few seconds while he takes a photograph. And then the fish is gone.

"That's my tarpon tarpon," I exult. "That's my proper tarpon. And, see, I caught it with you. Just as I told you I would. Now, we can all relax."

"About a fifty-pounder," Jeffrey says. I'm delighted it was not larger. I am truly weary.

Jeffrey is full of congratulations. Bubbling. But he still ponders the why of the unusually restless, leaping mass of tarpon: a sight, he tells me, he has seldom seen.

"I think I know why those fish were so excited," Jeffrey explains, looking at the puzzle precisely as he looks at each dawn, each day, each life. "I think they were jumping with joy. They'd been traveling through that storm and when they saw the Marquesas they knew they were close to home. They were rejoicing," he says. "They were dancing with joy."

And, each in our own way, so are both of us as Jeffrey points the bow toward Boca Grande Channel for our fast ride home.